D0057031

Love Parisienne

Love Parisienne

THE FRENCH WOMAN'S GUIDE TO LOVE AND PASSION

Florence Besson

Eva Amor

Claire Steinlen

Illustrations by Sophie Griotto

CHRONICLE BOOKS

SAN FRANCISCO

First published in the United States of America in 2018 by Chronicle Books LLC.

First published in France in 2016 by Éditions Michel Lafon.

Library of Congress Cataloging-in-Publication Data
Names: Besson, Florence, author. | Amor, Eva, author. | Steinlen, Claire, author.
Title: Love Parisienne : the French woman's guide to love and passion / Florence Besson, Eva Amor, Claire Steinlen.
Other titles: Amour a la Parisienne. English
Description: San Francisco : Chronicle Books, 2018. | "First published in France in 2016 by Michel Lafon."
Identifiers: LCCN 2016050311 | ISBN 9781452162782 (hc : alk. paper)
Subjects: LCSH: Man-woman relationships. | Sexual attraction. | Interpersonal attraction. | Interpersonal relations. | Single women.
Classification: LCC HQ801 .B492413 2018 | DDC 306.7—dc23 LC record available at https://lccn.loc.gov/2016050311

Manufactured in China

Design concept by Le BDAG.

Illustrations by Sophie Griotto.

10 9 8 7 6 5 4 3 2 1

Chronicle Books LLC
680 Second Street
San Francisco, California 94107
www.chroniclebooks.com

*"Why, oh, why do I love Paris?
Because my love is near."*

—COLE PORTER, AS SUNG BY ELLA FITZGERALD

CONTENTS

Part 2
ENCORE! ENCORE! STILL TOGETHER!

Part 3

YEARS OF HAPPINESS!

PREFACE

Once upon a time, fortune-tellers would haunt the trains of the Paris metro promising "eternal love, good fortune, and a driver's license." Alas, we cannot promise eternal love. But still we are ambitious! We are Parisian women, after all! And what we adore is romance. Love that starts in springtime in Paris. Love that brings a racing heart and shining eyes, with no thought of tomorrow. We want to celebrate joy in these pages. Joy in living, in making love, in being in a couple. You will not find any exact formulas here. Just common sense! Real advice, tested and approved by scores of Parisian women, les Parisiennes.

Our book is divided into three parts—having fun (Fleeting Pleasures), meeting (Encore! Encore! Still Together!), and experiencing long-lasting love (Years of Happiness!)—and it contains dozens of tips, time-tested advice, and reexamined clichés, plus addresses and lists to make your love affairs into a celebration with Paris as a backdrop. The sidebars sprinkled throughout—"Parisian Tips" and "Les Secrets d'une Parisienne"—provide inspiration for how to love like a Parisian woman, from places to kiss, to where to go for an impulsive romantic getaway. Whether you know Paris already or just have dreams of visiting it, let this book be your guide to romance.

"Poor are the larks that make love only in the spring," said the seventeenth-century French freethinker Ninon de Lenclos. Not so for the Parisienne! For her there are no taboos and no morality. For la Parisienne, life is an adventure she lives to the fullest, freely, without ever missing a beat and with (among others) gorgeous Parisian men as partners in the game. Her elegance is her imagination. Her courtesy is her lightness of spirit. Her style comes from the fact that she is all women rolled into one—daring to embody every role from Marie Antoinette to Brigitte Bardot, ever ready for the next wild experience.

All of Paris and all Parisians know how to love. From the classic films *À bout de souffle* to *Last Tango in Paris*, the city is a backdrop to *amour*. Every paving stone bears the memory of a racing pulse; every street is filled with memories of real or imagined affairs of the heart, a fling or a passion; and every bridge is a bridge of poets' sighs. In Paris, wrote Baudelaire, it is always "time to get drunk, for wine, for poetry, for virtue . . ." and also for freedom and for kisses.

We love everything in Paris. Even our bad moods, even our indifference, even—and this is a problem—our broken hearts. Suffering has its place in deepening our souls, but we believe in more joy! Our fervent hope is that this book will give you all you need to see "*la vie en rose*"!

– Florence Besson

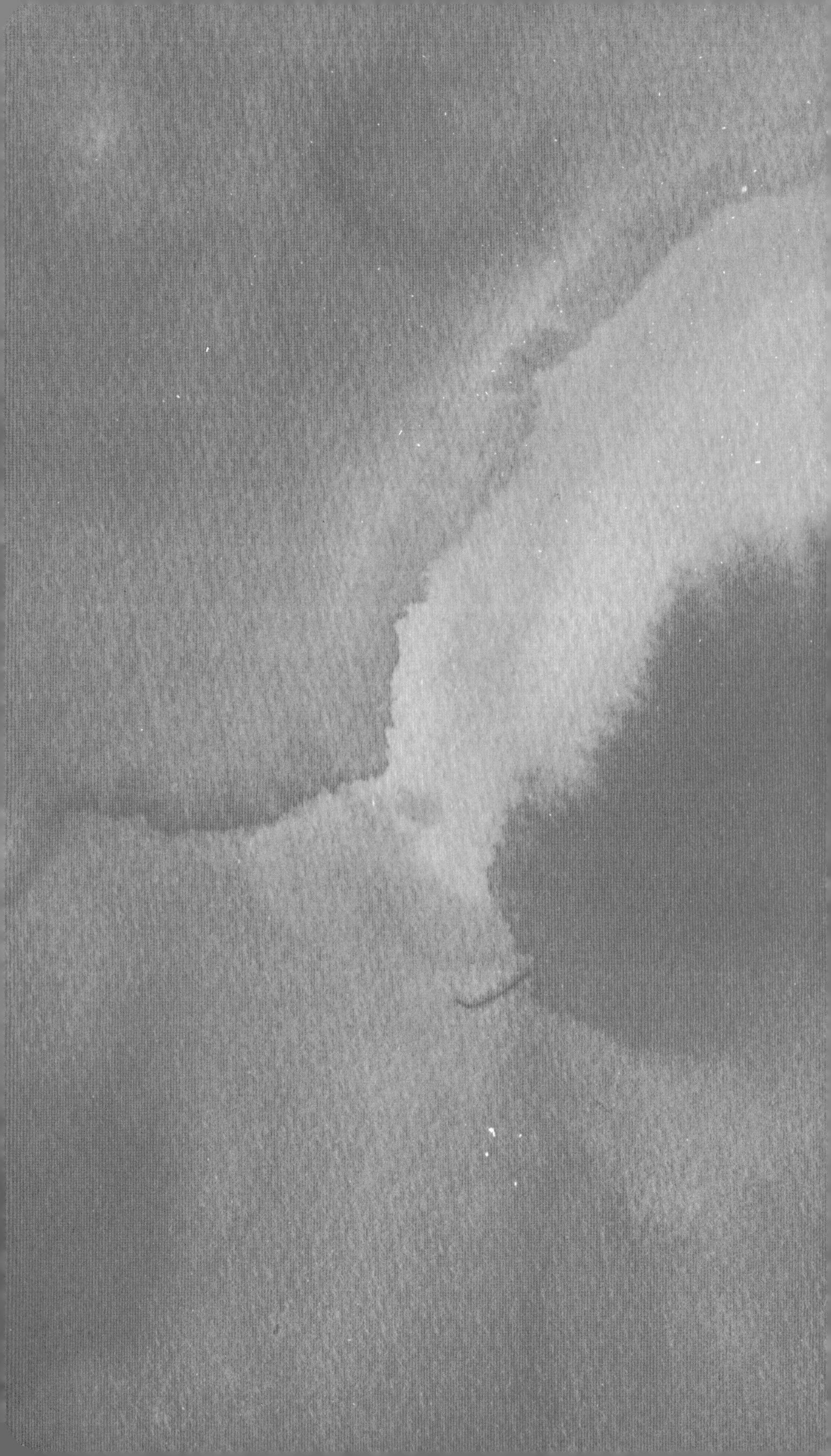

PART 1

Fleeting pleasures

A fleeting pleasure is an evening on the banks of the Seine with a handsome Italian who whispers sweet nothings into your ear. Or three scorching summer days with a colleague on top of office photocopiers that have never seen anything like it; or a mad hour with an ex-partner in the middle of the afternoon; or a week with a man, as yet unknown, who makes your heart race, and the hope that it will go on and on and on.

When you're single in Paris, life becomes a blank page of possibilities, with adventure just around every corner: eroticism for a day or a night, a brief romance, a love story waiting to happen. But whatever the new experience, the important thing is that it makes you happy and that you immerse yourself in it as fully as Louis XV's famous mistress Madame de Pompadour: being romantic but street-smart, free and playful, headstrong and independent. In short, the way Parisians drive—insanely, perhaps, but with lots of style!

So how can you enjoy this very particular method of loving à la Parisienne, whether it's getting a stranger into your bed, sharing a first dinner, savoring the first successful night, or taking or not taking a call? These are the questions! Take a seat at a terrace café, order a glass of Chablis or an apricot juice, and dip into this section as you would relish the beginnings of a love story. Life is beautiful—and you are too!

To love or not to love?

Parisian Tip

THE JEAN-PAUL SARTRE

Yes, we're in Paris, so let's begin with a little philosophy! Sartre said something that is really pretty wise: "Existence precedes essence." Very (very) roughly, that means: Look at yourself, observe what gives you pleasure, go where you feel happy, and you will know who you are (and who you like)! If that shocks people, blame Jean-Paul.

When it comes to love, you sometimes feel as if you just don't know what you're doing. You may feel that finding a guy—if only a decent one—is a bit like making slow-cooked lamb: too complicated! You find yourself wandering the streets feeling envy for the lovers kissing on benches while you hum a sad love song about heartbreak and loneliness. And yet, and yet . . . you dream of love, real love, true love, and of a hot guy.

So, here is the first rule of love: Listen to yourself. Ask yourself what you really want. Sometimes you just want to have fun—and that's absolutely fine! Enjoy yourself without guilt. Paris is also made for that.

And if you are dreaming of real love? Be careful: You need to be wise with your time and energy. So don't be under any illusions about him or about yourself: If what you like is bars packed with budding artists, don't waste your time with futile fantasies about socialites at a five-star Plaza Athénée hotel!

GOLDEN RULE: Know yourself! Stop comparing yourself to other people. Dare to be who you are, with your contradictions, your craziness, and your strange tastes. Look at your friends who are in relationships: Sometimes their choice of partner makes no sense to you. So forget the perfect man. What matters is your happiness!

I've forgotten how to hit on someone.

Never mind! Best not to throw out pickup lines like "Do you know how beautiful your eyes are?" to every passerby. Yes, take all the advice you can get about leaving your comfort zone (and your neighborhood, or arrondissement!). To parrot Georges Danton's famous words during the French Revolution, "We must dare, and dare again, and go on daring!" But don't lose your head! Techniques for hitting on someone, for both men and women, will get you nowhere. It is still better for you to wait to be approached.

Men are primitive? Indeed, and so much the better—so are you. We are nothing more than two animals on a small planet, two *Homo pseudo-erectis* impatient to rediscover fire. Let him play the caveman. Or let him believe he approached you, when, in fact, it was you who maneuvered it all.

GOLDEN RULE:
No frontal attacks. A few pointed looks, a laugh, a gesture replacing a stray lock of hair, that's all! You may be an independent, free woman, but for once you let someone else make the first move and you play the game. That's the fundamental rule!

Parisian Tip

NOTRE DAME FROM BEHIND!

Have you ever admired Notre Dame from behind? Stand on the Archevêché Bridge and get lost in admiration: those vaults rising up above the lime trees and horse chestnuts, those pointed arches, those aisles, those flanges, those columns, those towering abutments, those spires! Take inspiration from the immortal lady by turning your back on the guy and letting yourself be admired from behind (all the better to turn round again).

oulangerie Patisse
BOULANGER

Where do you find him?

Find your pleasures wherever you're happy, anywhere that gives you a kick. You just want an exotic night to file away in your memories? Then live out your digressions with a handsome tourist at the top of the Eiffel Tower, a PhD student on the paths of the Luxembourg Garden, or even an actor on the sofa of a flashy club on the Champs Élysées.

And finding the right one? Or rather one of the right ones, because we hate the idea that there is only one Louboutin that fits your foot? He may even be right under your nose. At the bus stop, at a luxury department store, or as you moan, "There aren't any taxis!" outside the nightclub one evening. A real meeting is shared by three: you, him, and a social place that you both enjoy. Without sharing a sense of place, it won't last. Which is not to say you can't find fleeting pleasures in a strange place! In short, open your eyes: The elusive specimen is often closer than you think.

GOLDEN RULE:

Be sexy everywhere! In the bistro or the movies, at the grocery store or the airport. Always cool and always prepared. That is the secret of Parisian style. So no Uggs or sequined tops—you need to adopt a quietly seductive style, a look that works as much for going out to pick up some bread as for ascending to seventh heaven. Coco Chanel always used to say to her seamstresses, "Never leave the house without looking perfect, my dear—it might be the day you find love!"

know his habitat!

In France we say "Impossible n'est pas Français"—in other words, "impossible" is not a Parisienne midset. But we do use common sense: You don't look for a hipster near the swanky Muette metro station or a banker at the flea market.

Here's a little map of Paris arrondissements to inspire you to look for your type in the right neighborhood—so you don't have to wander around for too long!

1ST A communications king • An elderly lawyer • A celebrity

2ND A realtor who's a bit of a womanizer but who dreams of marrying and having lots of kids • A DJ who at the moment is mainly a sales clerk at the fashionable men's clothing store AMI • A fashion photographer

3RD A journalist who'd really like to shack up with someone, but who isn't really sure . . . • An American staying in an Airbnb

4TH A bisexual interior decorator • A left-wing politician disguising his wealth • A rather famous sports coach

5TH A divorced literature professor who takes his children to the Jardin des Plantes . . . and is a bit of a dinosaur • Someone in cinema • A house-sharing student

6TH A writer who likes to look at himself in the mirrors of the Café de Flore • A publisher who loves literature • A young civil servant who's already bald

7TH A business lawyer, perhaps married—at least to his smartphone • An Italian collector • A newly rich journalist

8TH An elderly producer who's a reluctant clubber and loves women but already has lots of children • A gigolo • A guy who's started a business—it's not clear in what—that is doing well

9TH A young restaurateur just arrived from the Basque country with a very high profile and who is handsome, free, full of pep, and all the rage • A trendsetter who's in a relationship—depending on the time of day • A pianist

10TH A political activist, passionate about his cause and about anything that moves • A sociologist who drives you crazy going on about Pierre Bourdieu

11TH A student who needs a grant and lots of sex • A single dad who talks about the stock exchange and sex • A previous candidate on the cooking program *Top Chef*

12TH A nice dentist • A jazz musician! • A retiree who likes to watch the swans in the public park

13TH A nice, single hypnotherapist—great for finally giving up smoking • A medical intern at the Val-de-Grâce hospital • A composer who has a home in the trendy Butte-aux-Cailles neighborhood, paid for in cash after his big hit

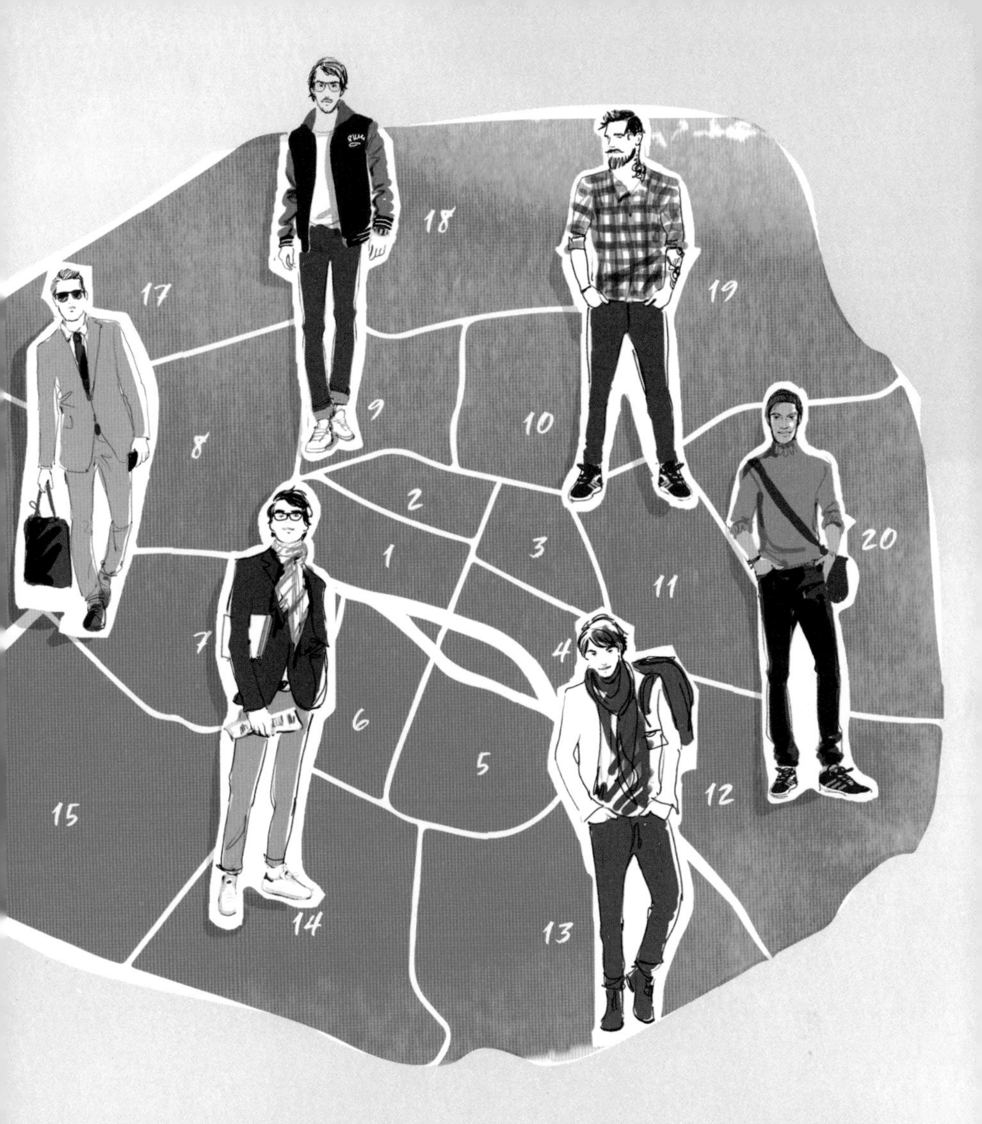

14TH A bartender, free during the day • A geek

15TH A climbing instructor, recently descended from the Alps and in search of a woman • An office colleague • Your cousin and the men who vaguely resemble him

16TH A family man who is not so faithful • A former party animal • An aristocrat who lives with his mother

17TH An ambitious young guy in finance, divorced with a child, as risky as a hedge fund • A bourgeois who thinks he is a "bourgeois bohemian" because he lives in the fashionable Batignolles neighborhood

18TH A successful actor, to test for an evening if you have the heart to climb up to Montmartre • An artistic director whose apartment is "really very nice" • An advertising man who is fiftysomething . . . and looks it

19TH A failed actor, needing to be pampered • A construction worker • A crazy Argentinian who's crazy about you

20TH A ceramics artist who is funny and gifted with his hands • A deacon who works at a Catholic charity • An ultra-heady multimedia artist

Dressing for the first date . . .

You're already an hour late, and you've got nothing to wear? Of course you have. Just go for the light touch, a suggestion rather than statement . . . sexy without saying so. Nothing predictable! Simple lines, a sleeveless T-shirt with bare shoulders, a white shirt giving a glimpse of black bra.

Underneath? Aim for your target: jeans for the hipster and a skirt for the business lawyer; heels for the man in finance and flats for the up-and-coming artist. Take note: heels with a miniskirt are a definite no (too "exotic dancer with an excessive libido") but obligatory if he is over forty-two (unless he is as short as France's recent presidents). The heels should never be too high—the aim is to seduce, not put yourself on display.

GOLDEN RULE:
Reveal only a little. Consider François Truffaut's film *The Man Who Loved Women,* about a man who was capable of fantasizing for hours about a piece of calf glimpsed in the street. Think of Romy Schneider before she dives into the water in the film *The Swimming Pool* and of her dresses revealing just a shoulder or a bare back. You don't need to display your cleavage or underwear; you can have a sensible blouse with just the top buttons undone. You don't have to dress like a dancer at the Crazy Horse cabaret to drive him crazy!

THE MEN LIKE FEMMES FATALES CLICHÉ

Yes, sometimes men do like women dressed as femmes fatales, but what really seduces them is femininity. No need to arm yourself with a military arsenal of costume effects—heels + skirt + plunging neckline—which, when all is said and done, is very aggressive and even disturbing. Put the emphasis on simplicity. Men like outfits they can understand. A skirt that gives a glimpse of leg (soon to be stretched out in bed with him!), or subtle cleavage that hints at the sacred treasure that lies beneath. Parisienne style is obvious chic and sobriety. Stay low-key.

Quick, I need an outfit for tonight!

Where a Parisienne goes for a last-minute ensemble

Addresses

LE BON MARCHÉ: Housed in the famous building with four pointed corners and with lots of relatively affordable smaller labels. Recent favorites: Bellerose, Gat Rimon.
24, rue de Sèvres, 75007 Paris.

And if you still haven't found what you're looking for, dash across the street to:

BRAND BAZAR: A Left Bank "label melting pot": two levels bringing together big-label clothes (Carven) and young designers (Sœur, Reiko, Momoni).
33, rue de Sèvres, 75007 Paris.

West of the capital, LE 66 ÉLYSÉE, on the Champs Élysées, offers a carefully chosen but broad selection with Majestic Fluid T-shirts, romantic dresses by Mes Demoiselles, and auspiciously named Catch Me Maybe clutch purses.

CENTRE COMMERCIAL: A "bourgeois bohemian" concept store decorated in white, wood, and antiquey furniture for chic shopping. Look for Roseanna slips, Paraboots, Larose hats, striped ponchos designed by La Méricaine, or adorable sailing dresses from Saint James.
2, rue de Marseille, 75010 Paris. Tel: 01 42 02 26 08.

And, of course, there's always ZARA or the H&M chic labels & OTHER STORIES and COS, all places where you can find something fun and sexy without overdoing it.

For the eco-minded

If you want to recycle, conserve the planet, and improve the conditions of textile workers, go to:

KILIWATCH: A Parisian haunt for vintage fashion where you can unearth a fur hat, a little leather jacket, or a silk blouse.
64, rue Tiquetonne, 75002 Paris. Tel: 01 42 21 17 37. www.kiliwatch.fr

NOIR KENNEDY: A vintage rock boutique and the ideal place to pick up Cheap Monday jeans, rock T-shirts, beautiful leather boots, or secondhand clothes.
22, rue du Roi de Sicile, 75004 Paris. Tel: 01 44 61 30 90.

On the web

VESTIAIRE COLLECTIVE: This website is all the rage; use it when you want to buy yourself that little Chanel bag your wardrobe is missing or the Classic bag from Céline you really like, for much less than in a shop. You post an alert and as soon as a fashionista puts one up for sale, you grab the opportunity. Experts guarantee the authenticity of the products.
www.vestiairecollective.com

I met him at Les Bains nightclub. Can it work?

Of course it can work! But it all depends on how you approach things. You must be cautious. For example, if you met this young man at Les Bains, the legendary Paris club/swimming pool, it means you're both cool but maybe he wants to have fun—but not just with you! You're there supposedly to splash around with your friends, but deep down you really wanted to flirt. Go on, go crazy, but just remember that you can't expect anything more from this guy (who's giving it all he's got on the dance floor) than a wild fling in the swimming pool: an erotic dive, as it were. Anything more, if you like each other, would be icing on the cake. It's not just womanizers who go to nightclubs—you and your best friends are also there, after all.

GOLDEN RULE:

The truth and nothing but the truth! It can't be repeated too often: The most important thing is to be honest with yourself. If you dive into these scorching waters with a stranger, it's because you're dying for him to put his hands on your breasts and that's all. If you feel in the mood for a quick plunge, free of regret or remorse, go for it—and remember that many people only fantasize about such aquatic evenings!

THE FREUDIAN CLICHÉ: FOLLOW YOUR DESIRE

The ever-intellectual Parisienne calls on the father of psychoanalysis: "Listen to yourself, follow your desire," therapists seem to say. But you have to know what your desire is! Are you certain you want just to have sex with this guy? Or do you think, in an out-and-out bit of maneuvering, that the shortest path to his heart is via his bed? Really listen to yourself, not to what you desire in the moment but to your deepest wishes—and don't feel you've got to be either a nun or a porn star. To find his heart, first follow your own.

The tricky phone number question

It's the big question. It's crazy how just a few numbers can create an equation with so many unknowns. Yet the answer is simple: Any Parisian well-versed in the art of flirtation knows offering your phone number before you've been asked for it is simply not done. And what if he doesn't request it? If he wants to, he'll find it out. Like you, the man is intelligent.

GOLDEN RULE:

Actually, there are three rules about texting:

1 Reply to his messages but avoid starting conversations yourself too often. Even if you are dying to—because you've already downed five of them—never send an "I was drinking a spritzer and I thought of you . . ."

2 Try to limit the number of texts you exchange. We are beyond rapid-fire exchanges ending with a "What are you eating?" Don't impoverish dialogue by thinking you have to go on with the back-and-forth.

3 If you're over fifteen, avoid smileys, although with the proviso that you are never too old to go crazy with a unicorn or a little dolphin as "proof" of your affection.

THE NOVELIST CLICHÉ

Let's be clear: Like every Paris inhabitant, you feel there is a writer in you. That's good. But for pity's sake, don't launch into romantic/mysterious texts along the lines of "You're so special . . ." or "I want so much to . . ." or even "If you knew . . . ," which leave the reader incapable of a response! Also to be avoided is the relentlessly comic text. It's true that men like women with a sense of humor, but they don't want to be constantly teased.

He's my boss! He's as old as my father and even has the same first name.

He can't be far from age sixty, he's called Jean-Pierre, and he's your boss: three reasons not to launch into anything with him. And yet you dive under the desk and act out a naughty secretary's fantasy. What *are* you thinking? To each her own!

The problem? First, France is a Latin, macho country. People might criticize you, thinking you're trying to sleep your way to the top, not knowing it's you who's on the top! Just be sure you really are attracted to this fiftysomething who is going a bit gray. You don't want to be seduced by his high office rather than the man himself.

So, because he is the boss, you remain professional: Retain your perspective and your cool, keep a clear head, and, above all, keep your distance. While you might not be scared of taboos, you have principles and you won't do anything to compromise a job you love. Or even just the atmosphere in the office. On the other hand, you play the oldie card all the way. Don't let him accompany you to nightclubs to relive his youth—you're not his Botox.

GOLDEN RULE: Don't be a nursing aide. An old scoundrel is acceptable—but if he's an old fogy you should get out of there! And refuse any mentor-pupil relationship with an older man who gives advice because he's not capable of doing much else anymore. Vintage sex is okay but a paternalistic lover with outdated values is not!

He's a bit of a loser.

He's an actor but things have not really taken off yet, so, in the meantime, he's playing an uprooted tree in an ultracontemporary (and very obscure) theater. He had been writing a screenplay about his ex-wife for the past five years but it was making him depressed so he gave it up . . . He's a waiter but his thing is music and he plans to create a group with a friend who's lending him an apartment and money . . . In short, on the face of it, you would be well advised to head for the hills and keep on running!

And yet . . . Isn't it beautiful that this man has the time to take the time? That, while you're sick to death of traffic jams or the jam-packed metro with the song "La Vie en Rose" played nonstop on an accordion, he can stroll around reciting poetic verses?

So why deprive yourself? If he isn't too depressed, say good-bye to money and enjoy this guy's genetic jackpot, with his well-made body and face. Go ahead: dive into this adventure! Here's a lover who will run you a bath and then get inside it to welcome you in person, having already perhaps drafted a screenplay or composed a new ballad. In any event, he won't ask if you've sent off the documents for the car insurance.

Hello to sleepless nights reciting Baudelaire's poetry, getting drunk, scaling the Sacré Coeur at night, endless discussions, mussels and French fries at five o'clock in the morning at a 24/7 brasserie. And if the gypsy charm starts to evaporate and the beautiful bird starts to lose a bit of its plumage or even to take a nosedive and flop to earth, you can let your shooting star whizz past. You'll be exhausted and relieved!

GOLDEN RULE:
Okay, he hasn't got a dime to his name but that's certainly not a reason to subsidize him! You are neither his mother nor his nurse. If he's really good, he will know that a simple plate of pasta, prepared sweetly and with love, can be a dish fit for a king, that a small paperback can be a great success, and that taking off his old, ripped jeans can make you wild with desire!

He's a star!

You've hung around the upscale nightclubs for so long, you've ended up French-kissing a Hollywood star on the dance floor. Bravo, you have now entered the Flirtation Hall of Fame—"Welcome, celebrity hunter!"—alongside Céline Balitran (four years with George Clooney after he hit on her in a Champs Élysées bar), François-Henri Pinault (nearly ten years with Salma Hayek after love at first sight in Venice), and the amazing Micheline Roquebrune (forty years with Sean Connery, the handsomest James Bond after encountering him on a golf course in Morocco).

But, like a good Parisian, you run into stars all the time—at the bakery buying your bread or at your yoga class—so don't be fazed by it, or at least act as if you don't recognize him. Best of all? Get him confused with another celeb—it shows that you couldn't care less about his celebrity!

GOLDEN RULE:
Keep a souvenir. Not staged photos, not a child—a souvenir. A diamond necklace, Mickey Mouse slippers (the star stayed young at heart), whatever. Something you might want to show your grandchildren one day.

Public kisses

Paris's best places to kiss in public

Challenge him to a game of pétanque in the PLACE DAUPHINE, a fun, quirky date.

Stroll hand-in-hand through the many Parisian covered passageways—among the capital's architectural curiosities—most of them close to or even joining each other: VÉRO-DODAT, VIVIENNE, and COLBERT malls. Take in the brasserie in the Colbert mall, Le Grand Colbert, a listed historical monument that regularly appears on the big screen; the Passage du Grand Cerf, filmed in Louis Malle's *Zazie dans le metro*; and the Passage des Panoramas, full of restaurants and charming cafés in the heart of the 2nd arrondissement.

Go with him to see the CITÉ INTERNATIONALE UNIVERSITAIRE in the 14th arrondissement, opposite the Parc Montsouris. This is a magnificent place, little known by Parisians; together you can explore the huge garden and the buildings modeled on structures from all over the world with their motley architectural styles. The International House, equipped with a swimming pool and theater, was funded by John D. Rockefeller, Jr. The Swiss and Franco-Brazilian foundations were designed by Le Corbusier.

If the weather is fine, have a picnic at VERSAILLES or in the Bois de Boulogne, where you can take the opportunity to ride in a boat. Otherwise, have a cuddly nap in the Place des Vosges or in the Palais-Royal gardens, or sip a mint syrup with water on the chairs of the Luxembourg Garden.

If it's overcast, take a stroll through the botanical garden LES SERRES D'AUTEUIL, created in 1761 under Louis XV, with its magnificent French-style flowerbeds. Then, if you are in the mood for reciting poetry, make your way to the neighboring Square des Poètes, with its slabs inscribed with verses from famous poets. For ultraromantics only!
1, avenue Gordon Bennett, 75016 Paris, and 3, avenue de la Porte d'Auteuil

Private kisses

Paris's best places to kiss in private

Most famous

Reserve for your exclusive use one of the private rooms of the LAPÉROUSE restaurant, location of romantic trysts in the nineteenth century. The courtesans would engrave their names on the mirrors with the diamonds their lovers had just given them, thereby checking whether they were authentic. Kate Moss imitated them by engraving *It's 2 late 2 go 2 bed* on the bar mirror!
51, quai des Grands Augustins, 75006. Tel: 01 43 26 68 04. www.laperouse.com

Most glamorous

L'OISEAU BLANC is a restaurant situated on the sixth floor of the Peninsula Paris hotel that gives a panoramic view of the most beautiful Parisian monuments. Few people know, however, that here the perfect lovers' table is to be found facing away from the room and toward the Eiffel Tower. You dine as a threesome with the Iron Lady, in complete privacy. Even more VIP: the restaurant rooftop, a mini-mini-terrace that can accommodate a table beneath the stars.
19, avenue Kléber, 75116. Tel: 01 58 12 67 30. www.peninsula.com

Most historic

LE PHARAMOND, a restaurant in a listed historical monument, was opened in 1832 by Alexandre Pharamond, who delighted Parisians with his baked tripes from Calvados. In the little private rooms that can be hired for two, where former president François Mitterrand and his mistress Anne Pingeot used to go, one can still encounter the ghosts of Clemenceau and Hemingway.
24, rue de la Grande Truanderie, 75001

Most original

Treat yourself to a ride on a PONTOON BOAT, a small pleasure craft that allows lovers to make a little getaway with a skipper and a bottle of champagne.
34, quai d'Austerlitz, 75013. Tel: 06 50 22 90 65. www.greenriver-paris.fr

Sex on the first date?

There are no absolute rules. From eighteenth-century feminist Olympe de Gouges to Simone de Beauvoir, you have plenty of liberated, avant-garde revolutionary female models to use as inspiration if you feel like saying, "I'll do as I please." However, in 90 percent of cases, "No" remains the best response. With all due respect, your grandmother's advice on the subject has proved its worth more than that given by your girlfriends after three glasses of Sancerre. And, even in the twenty-first century, it is proven beyond doubt that making him wait two or three dates is really worth it, if only to make certain you really do find him attractive!

Being romantic is a bit like music in films—it makes your heart beat faster. It's not necessarily your sex-mad side—like the queen of Nesle's Tower (that medieval princess who was said to bring lovers up to her tower before throwing them into the Seine)—but your desire for a real love affair that will make him want it too.

GOLDEN RULE:
If you've said yes, you always go to his place. You take his condoms (you don't have any hanging around at the bottom of your bag) and you depart in the middle of the night on tiptoe, leaving the memory of your evening together untouched.

He wanted to spank me!

Nothing is taboo to the Parisienne . . . but you don't want to begin with an S&M film, all the same. You were secretly dreaming of a café under the roses of the Museum of Romantic Life—and here you are feeling like you've picked up someone who's escaped from a sex club? It's ugly. If this man doesn't want to wait or make the effort to find out something about you before launching you into the *Story of O*, it means he's interested only in a bit of casual sex. Tonight he's with you; and tomorrow?

GOLDEN RULE: Whatever happens, never forget that the first night might be the last. If so, and you're not going to see each other again, then you give everything without a second thought, saying to yourself, "Merci beaucoup!"

So, unless you've been together for six months or are crazy about riding crops being misused, get out of there! Men, too, usually prefer less exhausting first evenings. You'll have more than enough time to resort to fantasies when things start to get a little boring: Keep it in reserve.

But think about this: When his hand patted your bottom while he uttered some rather daring and dirty words, what did you feel deep down? A little frisson? It's not impossible. It's a curious feeling the first time, but if he did it on the spur of the moment and doesn't seem like a pro out of a video, well, it means he was able to predict your most secret desires . . . which is a promising sign!

THE TABATHA CASH CLICHÉ

Do you feel like you're doing acrobatic rock? That you are in the Olympic games in the middle of a more or less artistically choreographed skating routine and that, at the end, you'll be graded a 5.2? You are victim of the Tabatha Cash cliché, named after the famous French porn heroine. No, doing bizarre contortions won't make you happy. Nor will accessories. Nor the arrival of a whole grocery store in the bed, from chocolate spread to whipped cream. On the first night, less is more! Find out about each other, sniff each other, play on each other's heartstrings. You've got the rest of your lives to invite friends in.

How to undress

Parisian Tip

THE CROISSANT TRICK

You are at his place or he is at yours, and you feel like two minutes alone? Quick! Send him to buy croissants. You'll have just enough time to brush your teeth in peace or quickly phone a friend . . . In the evening, the need adapts to fresh cream/spices/bread/champagne. Paris never sleeps; send him to the store!

He's arrived. He's here. In your home. In your room. "Help, I'm overweight!" you despair. Too overcome to keep a cool head, you smile as weirdly as Mona Lisa, you remember that pair of jeans you can no longer fit into, that astronomically expensive membership to that gym you never set foot in, and your overwhelming devotion to chouquette pastries. What then?

First: Does one need to point out that you don't do it in the pallid neon light of the bathroom but with dimmed lighting instead?

Second: Remember your teenage years. When you made love semidressed, you were in such a hurry. Do the same thing! If you wait until he really can't hold back any longer, rest assured he will not notice any of your minor faults.

Third: Both before and after making love, choose the most flattering positions and get out of bed naked underneath his shirt, adorned with a sheet and your dignity.

GOLDEN RULE:

Do not run into the bathroom, take a shower, put makeup on, and exchange your granny panties for the latest La Perla body! Go with the flow; he undresses you and you undress him (unless you're playing strip poker). You also don't fold your clothes and you don't go brush your teeth. Abandon yourself to the moment. And if, the following day, you find your panties on the mantelpiece—fantastic.

Undressing in style

Parisiennes turn to these chic stores for their undergarments

At the high priestess of style, Inès de la Fressange, who has opened LEFT BANK BOUTIQUE, a very "Rive Gauche" concept store in a former foundry, you can treasure-hunt for Fifi Chachnil lingerie, bustiers, and lace panties.
24, rue de Grenelle, 75007 Paris
www.inesdelafressange.fr

DÉMENT: This lingerie range created by Laetitia Schlumberger in somber colors (black, white, dark blue) is still very feminine, with the special feature of magnets hidden under little bows, allowing you to get undressed in the blink of an eye!
Divine Parisienne, 19, rue Guisarde, 75006 Paris.
www.lingerie-dement.com

SABBIA ROSA: This "boudoir boutique" with lingering fragrances houses marvelous, insanely chic, and 100 percent French creations of embroidered silk.
73 rue des Saints Pères, 75006 Paris.
Tel: 01 45 48 88 37.

CADOLLE: Its founder, Herminie Cadolle, embodies the courageous Parisienne: She took part with Louise Michel in the revolutionary events of the Paris Commune and invented the first brassiere. Perhaps the style you choose will resemble the one she presented to the Universal Exhibition of 1889—the event for which the Eiffel Tower was built!
255, rue Saint Honoré, 75001 Paris.
Tel: 01 42 60 38 37.
www.cadolle.fr

Oh dear, he was useless in bed.

Parisian Tip

A GLASS OF RED WINE . . . TO LOOSEN YOUR TONGUES

A glass is enough to remove inhibitions. His. Yours. To start whispering sweet nothings. "Yes, that's good," at first, soon followed by, "Yes, harder," or whatever takes your fancy. Everyone has their own vocabulary: Poet? "I love your apricot"; Scriptwriter? "I'm sure the neighbor is looking at us"; Romantic? "I could drown myself in you." It doesn't matter what you say, as long as you're intoxicated!

He's as handsome as a movie star and he had you reeling with desire when he held you against a streetlight at the corner, but on the living room couch he is about as irresistible as a soggy baguette . . . Never mind! Whether there was a series of clumsy fumblings, deathly boredom, an awkward size problem, or a downright breakdown in functioning, don't panic. Instead, you give up momentarily, telling yourself you have lost a battle but not the war.

Be careful, however: If it's really disastrous and you're not all that attached to this great clumsy oaf, remember that you're not Mother Teresa. You need to know when to walk on by. There's someone for everyone, and you can leave him to his defeat.

GOLDEN RULE: Above all, don't be frank! Never! At first, say nothing and do not grade the mistakes. Rome was not built in a day, nor was the Eiffel Tower erected in a moment. Encourage him. After all, it's flattering, he is overwhelmed, and to him you are a goddess. Take the upper hand. Sex is like wine; it gets better with time!

We slept together, and he doesn't call.

The worst thing is wasting time wondering why he hasn't called. The more you try to understand, the greater your risk of spending weeks weeping over a guy you don't even know! Don't listen to your girlfriends who gently mislead you. He doesn't ring because he doesn't want to, that's all there is to it! Forget about him and consider the next encounter.

Just because you spent the night together doesn't mean he's sworn undying love to you. Women may be liberated, but deep down we still believe that a night of sex equates to attaching a love lock to the Pont des Arts.

No, no, no! To help you get over it, the most courageous thing you can do is delete his number, or at least change his name on your mobile so you're not tempted to call him, or personalize his ring tone so your heart doesn't start racing every time a girlfriend texts you.

GOLDEN RULE:

Don't mess around with love. It's up to him to call, and not in three days' time! In Paris, people are always waiting: for the metro, for a taxi, in a movie queue . . . everyone has thirty seconds for a few words of love.

Parisian Tip

MY NIGHT AT THE MUSEUM

He doesn't want to spend another night or more days with you? No matter! You have Rodin, Delacroix, Poussin, Géricault, and countless other men, all fascinating in other ways, awaiting you for a nocturnal session at the Louvre. If you're going to be a single woman, you may as well be a smart one! (We recommend this instead of a wine-filled evening with a girlfriend, with its attendant risks of tears and a 4 a.m. phone call.)

THE MAMA CLICHÉ

"Men are big babies and you have to reassure them." Who says they need reassurance? Isn't it you reassuring yourself by calling him? Don't put yourself inside someone else's head—it's complicated enough in your own.

He calls!

You are quietly doing some work in your bed, in front of a roaring log fire, when suddenly "the" name is displayed on your phone. All at once, you feel like Joan of Arc in proud horsewoman mode, on her gold steed outside the Louvre: "Oh no, I won't answer, I'm not available at the drop of a hat!" Hardly!

Of course you answer. But not necessarily in a hurry. You adopt a kind, considerate, funny, and lighthearted tone . . . but you are not free to see him right away.

You're sorry but tonight you can't; you feel like staying at home for a sushi night with your favorite TV show because—even if it is not true—you were out at a swanky bar last night. But offer to meet him tomorrow night. Where? Neither somewhere with just the two of you, nor a formal date.

GOLDEN RULE:

Always let him be a step ahead. It's he who proposes, you who disposes! That way, you will always feel more confident and will be all the more seductive. If you are scared of harassing him like someone possessed, do a Javert—the bad guy in *Les Misérables* who threw himself into the river—and throw your phone in the Seine! It will do you good and it was time to change it anyway. For two days, you won't be contactable. He will have phoned twenty times and you will be radiant.

LES SECRETS D'UNE PARISIENNE:

Why doesn't he join you at the Rosa Bonheur bar under the Alexandre III bridge, where you have planned to have an aperitif with friends? Or at the opening of a gallery in the Marais, before going for a drink at the Georges restaurant on the top story of the Pompidou Center? What could be more romantic than reaching for a hand as you consider art together?

THE '70S CLICHÉ

We are equals, and a woman has the right to call. Yes, of course, but why would she? Do you know a single man, even the shyest, who won't take the first step when he's in love? If he really hasn't spotted you, go for it and get out your phone, but realize that you are starting out with one fewer card in your hand—and that you will need to protect yourself all the more afterward!

He sends dozens of texts but we never meet up.

Something's fishy. Here is a man who gets fired up all on his own, who sends you texts that say things like, "I'm going crazy thinking about you" or "Are you dressed right now?" or "I can't take this desire anymore, I'm going for a jog"—but who never suggests meeting or, when you do make plans, cancels all the time. His texts are like Facebook "likes": They are just distractions to help him pass the time. Worse, this may be a cover-up for the fact that he's got too many commitments to take it any further—or a wife.

So, beware. A real man knows what he wants and hopefully it's you. If he's not making time to see you, let him go.

GOLDEN RULE:
You may exchange millions of Tinder messages or texts on trivial subjects, but you quickly meet up. Do not measure his attachment by the number of his messages but rather by his actions. A guy who is really smitten will make the effort to see you in person! And so, poetic digital communications be damned, you have to become almost mathematical: 15 texts = 1 meeting. Otherwise, it's not worth it.

Surprise, he's returning to Buenos Aires tomorrow!

He's leaving. He only had a tourist visa? He must return to take care of the family tango club? In short, your love is literally flying away. Should you cry? Yes, of course. (See our list of the best places in Paris for that, page 109.) Believe it will last, despite everything? Hmm. Don't tell yourself, "It doesn't matter, I'll go and see him." Long-distance love doesn't work.

What is certain is that before he leaves, you will have to live as though you are in a film: "I love yous" on tourist riverboats, ardent kisses on the steps of Montmartre, rolling in the grass near the rose gardens in Bagatelle, spending the night in a suite at the luxurious Hotel Raphael—in short, your very own remake of *An American in Paris*! An affair is not less good because it is short rather than long. If it's short, it is all the more memorable!

GOLDEN RULE:
When it's a short-lived affair, throw caution to the wind! That contradicts other rules? Not at all: Strategy is a matter not of caution but of intelligence. Go for it—it will be a wonderful memory and you will be even more radiant as you walk down the street thinking of the love letters you are going to exchange with someone in Argentina or of that torrid night during which he muttered funny words in Spanish.

The first drink: Do I treat it like a job interview?

Of course you'll lie. He will, too. That first cocktail bar is your very own film studio, with each of you playing a role: "myself, in a slightly better version." His anecdotes, his frequent laughter, and his enthusiasm are designed to impress. But be careful not to embellish yourself too much. Don't list your qualities, assets, activities, and prestigious exes. You're not for sale. As La Rochefoucauld said: "We gain more by allowing ourselves to be seen as we are than by trying to seem what we are not."

So what do you talk about? About everything and nothing—on such evenings, words are merely appetizers, at least on the surface. What about putting out feelers to discover his tastes and express yours? For example: Your favorite city to escape to on impulse for a weekend. What he thinks of your mutual friends. (What he says about others says a lot about him.) And then there's always good old Parisian debates: Does the Left Bank–Right Bank rivalry still exist? You couldn't care less but you discuss away! The important thing is what lies behind the conversation and the good vibes you are very gently exchanging.

GOLDEN RULE:
Don't give your résumé! And if your stomach is still in knots after all this advice, repeat to yourself ten times on the way there that this man must say about you, "I'm crazy about her—she's made for me!" Don't get hung up on which is your most attractive profile. It might be your liking for camembert at breakfast that has him falling at your feet!

Parisian Playlist

Songs to listen to on the way to your first drink together

"Mon Manège à Moi" Étienne Daho
"Something About Us" Daft Punk
"Intoxicated" Martin Solveig
"When Love Takes Over" David Guetta
"Donner pour Donner" F. Gall & E. John
"Zou Bisou Bisou" Gillian Hills
"La Fièvre" NTM
"Moi Vouloir Toi" Françoise Hardy
"Lady" Modjo
"Une Femme Like You" K Maro
"Amoureuse" Véronique Sanson
"Sea, Sex and Sun" Serge Gainsbourg
"La Vie en Rose" Grace Jones
"Sensualité" Axelle Red
"Déshabillez-moi" Juliette Gréco
"Vertige de l'Amour" Bashung
"À Bouche que Veux-tu" Brigitte
"Dreams Are My Reality" Richard Sanderson
"Une Autre Histoire" Gérard Blanc
"J'attends l'Amour" Jenifer

I drank too much and blurted everything out!

Parisian Tip

THE HAM SANDWICH TRICK

You're going for a drink tonight . . . but you're scared you'll down a whole bottle, you're so stressed! Quick, run to the bakery to get a ham sandwich! You will be full and your stomach, that famous second brain, will send you signals of happiness and stop you from making a fool of yourself. If you are gluten-intolerant, swallow a boiled egg.

The stress, the knot in your stomach, the urge to get drunk straight away so you'll forget you've put the wrong shirt on, feeling overwhelmed and helpless at the way he looks at you, the wanting to be in his arms without further ado, and the anxiety about whether he will kiss you . . . You had agreed to meet at 7 p.m., in order to be able to escape with the pretext of a dinner party if it turned out to be a disaster. It wasn't: It's now midnight and all you've swallowed is three peanuts, a tiny slice of Comté cheese, and an entire bottle of Pouilly-Fuissé wine! You go home tipsy, regretting having shared that you are down to your last dime, that you were completely depressed two days ago, or even that you've bought a Japanese toilet for its divine heated seat.

If possible it is best to avoid unloading old neuroses, sad stories, and, lastly, red wine (blue lips minimize your recall abilities). But other than that, trust yourself—what could be worse than trying to be in control when it comes to love? You are alive, sensitive, carried away? All the better! Remain enthusiastic without being scared of silences (he will fill them) or of laughter for no reason (such elation is flattering)—in principle, he should be in the same state. You have the right to spend a pleasant moment in delightful company. Both of you are there to give a little tenderness. Repeat to yourself that phrase of Pope Jean Paul II, champion of love: "Be not afraid!"

GOLDEN RULE:

If you've unpacked your exes and your parents' divorce, above all don't try to apologize for it: "No, nothing at all, no, I regret nothing," sang Édith Piaf—and the same goes for you! Strictly forbidden is, "I'll call him to say I'm sorry." You have nothing to apologize for; you're wonderful! Is that clear?

BISTROT
de Tradition

First dinner at your place—store-bought sushi or a good home-cooked meal?

Oh là là! Above all, don't start getting overambitious. You are not a world-famous chef. And it's not the time to go hunting through those recipe books you've never even opened. You remain simple, like your look—low key!

It goes without saying that you only agree to him coming to your place if he has already invited you out to dinner . . . Now you have opted for a quiet evening at home. Okay, but how? With a good Italian pasta! Or a good plate of seafood—a female foodie licking her fingers after devouring a fresh oyster is sexy!

In short, you go to your upscale local grocer and tonight you will be nibbling . . . a man and crackers! Above all, nothing that smacks of "fine dining"! Do we need to remind you that he has not come for dinner?

GOLDEN RULE: Involve him. Tell him to bring what he wants, choose together, transform that "My God, I've got to make dinner" into an enthusiastic "We're doing something together!" And be sure not to set the table before he arrives: If you do, how will you be able to make love on it right away?

THE VERSAILLES CLICHÉ

Tonight, the famous hotelier Vatel will be delighting your palates! And the playwright Molière has written the script! And Béjart is the choreographer! Hang on . . . where do you think you are? No need to spend thousands, produce scintillating conversation, or put on a spectacular show worthy of Versailles. Forget pomp and circumstance: too exhausting. It's for him to pluck down the stars for you.

Recipe ideas

For the first dinner at home

If it's hot

You buy wild salmon or a ham to die for from your local butcher, served with baby or steamed potatoes—it's fun, agreeable, and needs no preparation!

All year round

You make a little appetizer platter to nibble, with good-quality smoked salmon, hummus, goat cheese, and a good Comté cheese—but no garlicky dips (foul breath) or tabouli salad (herbs in the teeth!) the first evening.

If he's under forty

Make a croque-monsieur—and you brave the innuendo (the name is derived from *croquer* ("to bite") and *monsieur* ("mister")! Buy some ready-made béchamel sauce, some good ham, and some good cheese. To be served with a Bibb lettuce cut in two as long as the leaves are not the dangerous kind (see the list of forbidden foods below!).

If he's over forty

Make your own good-quality, easy pasta, without tomato sauce. A very simple recipe: Dissolve a chicken stock cube in fresh cream and pour it over burning-hot short pasta (penne, farfalle, orecchiette). Serve with some beautiful tomatoes and you can even grate a truffle over it if you're feeling indulgent.

List of forbidden items!

Overly fatty sushi, any herb or salad that can get stuck between the teeth, spaghetti that is alluring only in *Lady and the Tramp*, garlic for reasons you know about, and dishes covered in sauce—not sexy!

He didn't pick up the tab.

Obviously, you get out your credit card—you're an independent woman—and obviously he appreciates the gesture. But obviously . . . it is out of the question for him to accept! Equality, okay, but gallantry above all. For dinner—and breakfast croissants—it's for him to pay. What if he's penniless? Forget the VIP table at the fashionable restaurant and go explore all the hole-in-the-wall Japanese restaurants until the bank has unfrozen his card. If you want to pay for him? Pay the waiter discreetly so the matter is out of his hands.

GOLDEN RULE: You are an extraordinary woman who earns her living and has no need of his money. But you do need his love—and love needs to be shown!

Where to take him?

For lunch

BRASSERIE FLOTTES: We adore this brasserie near the Tuileries for its vintage setting and its traditional Averyon recipes (not for its proximity to the Chanel store).
2, rue Cambon, 75001. Tel: 01 42 60 80 89. www.flottes.fr

BOUILLON CHARTIER: Just walking inside this legendary brasserie immediately plunges you into the nineteenth century. Even better, each dish costs around 10 euros!
7, rue du Faubourg Montmartre, 75009. Tel: 01 47 70 86 29. www.bouillon-chartier.com

Also the LAITERIE SAINTE CLOTILDE, 64, rue de Bellechasse, 75007; EDGAR, 31, rue d'Alexandrie, 75002; and the pizzeria IL BRIGANTE, 14, re du Roisseau 75018: the best pizza in Paris.

For dinner

RUE PAUL BERT: Together you can choose between a glass of wine and a platter of cheese at the Bistrot Paul Bert at number 18, the oysters of the Bistrot at number 22, and a fine piece of meat at the Argentinian restaurant Unico at number 15. 75011

CORETTA: A light, bright restaurant in the heart of the Batignolles with bay windows looking out onto the Martin Luther King park (the restaurant is named after King's wife). Modern fine dining.
151, rue Cardinet, 75017. Tel: 01 42 26 55 55. www.coretta.fr

PAVILLON PUEBLA: In the heart of the Buttes Chaumont Park (75019). In the evening, cross the park to enjoy pizzas and platters to share in this hunting lodge in the style of Napoleon III.

On paper it's perfect—but there is a but . . .

If you don't fall deeply in love straight away, so much the better—that can be a good sign. When you do fall in love, you will be fully conscious rather than bewitched. You will be truly enamored, seduced and delighted. Happy. And sure of your feelings.

At the same time, if you feel like you're in a bad play—in short, that you're going out with someone else's ideal man or with an abominable creation dreamed up by Stalinist advertisers (or even by your mother)—start running and escape this ideal son-in-law to nestle in the arms of that sizzling waiter or that slightly disreputable guy who makes you fantasize a hundred times more! People are sometimes tempted to have a relationship with someone who seems to check all the boxes but whom they already find boring. Just think of the efforts you will have to make to keep this "rational relationship" going, and how many more to find the courage to leave and finally be free to make the right choice. A man who is perfect on paper is like a loft in Les Invalides—chic but cold, like living life looking out at a tomb! So if you're not really happy or are even slightly depressed? Escape, right away. The first step toward happiness is to flee unhappiness! Obvious but true.

PS: This also goes for those women who think they're living a great love affair but do nothing but cry all day as they wait for him to call!

GOLDEN RULE:
Three weeks and that's it. After that, you listen to yourself! If you don't want to, you don't want to, and that's that! No circumstances oblige you to sacrifice your heart. Look at Cécilia Attias, who divorced Nicolas Sarkozy (while he was president) in her mid-fifties, or Eleanor of Aquitaine, who dumped a French king and gave half of France to England out of love. Be daring! Something so much better is waiting for you around the corner.

Parisian Tip

APPLE PASTRY

We Parisiennes love a good apple puff pastry. What is it we enjoy so much? The number of apples? The amount of flour? Of sugar? The fat? No, we love the expertly crafted mixture, which means that the same recipe made by luxury pâtissier Rodolphe Landemaine is much nicer than something created in a chemistry lab. Well, a man is like a cake. The ingredients do not matter—handsome, intelligent, funny, cultivated, affectionate—what matters in the end is your particular taste!

To be honest, his body is really odd.

Parisian Tip

LUNCHEON IN THE PARK

Picnic on the grass, or enjoy lunch in a little bistro—it's more practical. That way, you have three hours (the time spent at lunch, in other words!) to really evaluate the product in the light of day. Afterward you go back to work and either forget all about him or stew with impatience to see him again that same evening.

By objective standards he is ugly. Or badly dressed. Or both. So what? Think of Brigitte Bardot, who fell for singer Serge Gainsbourg with his less-than-film-star looks and appearance! Or of Madame de Staël, who was ugly as sin but who managed to get the whole of Paris into her bed (and her salons) just with her conversation. His bad taste doesn't matter—you can give him a makeover in three minutes (see next entry)—nor does the fact that he doesn't have a torso like Ryan Gosling. Think of Leonardo DiCaprio: It's crazy how one body can do so many different things. (There will be plenty of time to get him on the right track.)

The truth is, you don't trust yourself. Because you have waited for love, you ask yourself whether you will find yourself like the heron in the fable by La Fontaine, forced to make do with a snail because you turned your nose up at pike . . . Nonsense! You are too romantic for that. What matters is that feeling all hot and bothered in his presence, the way his skin attracts your skin, his fingers set all your senses alight, his mouth burns on your neck, his intoxicating voice murmurs in your ear, those disturbing thoughts in your brain, and that he makes you laugh. That's all!

GOLDEN RULE: If you feel you have really fallen under his charm, forget any awkward details. Give him his chance and give yourself the chance to be surprised. In any case, as we have said, it is better not to find everything about him attractive—that way you will keep your head a (very little) bit more.

THE COSTES CLICHÉ

Paris's Costes restaurants are beautiful and glitzy but very expensive for what they are. The waitresses size you up with a very 1990s contempt that is the height of tackiness. Today, we have returned to what really matters: the essence of things. Think of Baudelaire—"Beauty is always bizarre"—and go for a being whose outer edges are rather rough but who is gorgeous on the inside—like a Ferrero Rocher chocolate!

Where to get him a makeover

If your man needs a bit of style help, find inspiration in these go-to Parisian stores

STEP 1: IF YOU'VE REALLY GOT YOUR WORK CUT OUT

You've got work to do if he thinks skinny trousers are still where it's at—or if he has no opinion on the subject.

APC: Otherwise known as the ABC of fashion.

Here you will find basic jeans in Japanese denim (selvedge) with a very good price/quality ratio and a whole collection of sweaters that will transform absolutely anyone into a handsome hunk.

Purists should go to rue Vieille du Temple, to ELEVATION STORE (twice as expensive as APC for the Rolls-Royce of jeans). The rest of the collection consists of timeless items with sober cuts and classic colors (beige chinos, striped sweaters, gray sweatshirts, and thick flannel shirts that will make him look more like a trusty woodcutter than an out-of-date hipster).

The men's department of BON MARCHÉ houses a selection of labels in a limited space with guaranteed efficacy: Balthazar, the house label, or De Fursac or Corneliani (more expensive) to give makeovers to lawyers and bankers. The latter need only go a few steps to rue Chomel to buy shoes (Caulaincourt Paris). The designer square also offers an exhaustive choice from J. Crew to Carven and from Acne Studios to Lanvin. At the end of the store is a selection of sneakers and also of swimming trunks, in case you plan to put the interested party into your suitcase this summer (Robinson les Bains, Orlebar Brown . . .).

MERCI: Avoid Colette, with its touristy crowd, and make your way instead to this fair-trade concept store (a share of the profits is given to charitable organizations) that is also as Parisian as they come. A fine selection of peacoats, sweatshirts, accessories, and several original labels such as Homecore. As a bonus, you will be near a thousand great places for predinner drinks . . . or a dinner for just the two of you!

STEP 2: HE NEEDS A HELPING HAND

AMI: Your new best friend. Attractive materials, sober colors, classic or oversize cuts for tops, slightly tapered fit for bottoms. A special mention for their jackets and coats, which are a great success. French rapper JoeyStarr is a fan of the three-quarter-length sheepskin, now a must-have!

MAISON KITSUNÉ: For an attractive teddy—*kitsuné* means "fox" in Japanese—that you won't find anywhere else than in Paris or the most chic places in Tokyo.

L'ÉCLAIREUR: A very enlightened fashion choice if you want to unearth a beautiful scarf or because he is longing to see the newest collection by Kanye West.

For geeks or those in a hurry, the MR PORTER app gives you the whole of men's fashion in one click, the male counterpart of our favorite site, Net-a-Porter.

A naughty rendezvous?

He's suggested you meet in a hotel bar—and here you are, just the two of you (the three old ladies and the two Saudi princes have disappeared), you're drunk on spritzers, and he asks: "Shall we take a room?"

The question in Brigitte Bardot's song goes through your head: "Do you want to or not?" But it's such fun to play the heroine! It makes for an exciting change, it's amusing, it's a magical place . . . obviously you say yes!

GOLDEN RULE:
Accept only if it's in a fantastic place. Not a motel in a run-down part of town! And you always refuse to meet him during the 10–11 a.m. or the 3–4 p.m. time slots . . . which are for women who are paid by the hour.

THE 5 O'CLOCK CLICHÉ

Who still has time to slip out of the office at 5 p.m. for a two-hour liaison? Nobody! Squeezing a naughty rendezvous into teatime, between an important meeting and a vital cocktail party, smacks more of hard work than relaxation. The five-to-seven has had its day. The noon-to-two slot has taken over. It's better for the figure and much easier to get past the boss.

Hotels for a five-to-seven

Unlike Japan and Brazil, France does not have a tradition of love hotels where you can rent a room by the hour—but the creative Parisienne can find a solution!

The site WWW.DAYUSE-HOTELS.COM offers rooms for the day: a bijou apartment next to the Opéra, a room with a view over Montmartre, or a suite under the roofs near Étoile.

In the romantic suite with a terrace and Jacuzzi at the FIVE HOTEL, you can take the champagne and massage option.
3, rue Flatters, 75005 Paris. www.thefivehotel.com

At VICE ET VERSA, Chantal Thomass designed the rooms using the inspiration of the seven deadly sins.
213, rue de la Croix Nivert, 75015 Paris. Tel: 01 55 76 55 55. www.viceversahotel.com

HÔTEL AMOUR: Admire fashionable clients and enjoy rooms you can rent by the hour, with photos of nudes and a flower-filled patio.
8, rue de Navarin, 75009 Paris. Tel: 01 48 78 31 80. www.hotelamourparis.fr

Or visit its big brother in the 10th, HÔTEL GRAND AMOUR at number 18 in the ironically named rue de la Fidélité.
Tel: 01 44 16 03 30.

A moment of madness? Go for one of the eight Parisian grand hotels. At the BRISTOL, we love the French-style gardens, the swimming pool on the terrace, and the two cats that wander around the sitting rooms.
12, rue du Faubourg St. Honoré, 75008. Tel: 01 53 43 43 00.

Strategy? Yes—but at the strategic moment!

Parisian Tip

THE CALLAS

When Maria Callas, that splendid Greek beauty with the golden voice and overwhelming style, was dumped like an old sock by Aristotle Onassis for an ex–first lady, what did she do? Did she go and weep at his door? Did she throw herself into the arms of the first president who came along to get revenge? No. She disappeared. She shut herself up behind the façade of a Haussmann building in the 16th arrondissement to get over her troubles and the loss of her voice (which had also made a run for it). And what happened? On his deathbed, Aristotle Onassis clutched the red Hermès cashmere blanket she had given him, a sign that he had never forgotten her. Absence never destroys true love!

They say the first three months of a love affair are all about marketing. You abandon yourself in bed, but otherwise you carefully observe how things are unfolding and you control yourself. You hatch plans.

Is that sad? Not at all! Love isn't war but it's better if you're armed. Take an Uber driver, for example. In principle, his GPS always tells him the best route. But what if there is a strike on? A demonstration? A fashion week causing gridlock? It's wise to have your own map open, so as to propose your own shortcuts ("Yes, it's a one-way street but it's very small!") and your own scenic routes. Well, it's the same with love: If he goes on telephone strike for a bit, gets into a bad mood over nothing, or is hit on by a Bulgarian supermodel, be strategic! Act indifferent when it looks like he might disappear, know how to make him jealous when necessary, bring out the big game in bed if you've got something he needs to forgive you for, and, why not, simper a little when you've got something to ask him.

GOLDEN RULE:
As far as possible, keep a cool head. Love is marvelous but for it to last, you cannot treat it as any old thing.

He's still on Tinder.

If he is openly seeing women other than you—well, he can get lost. In Paris, as soon as you kiss, you're an item. Maybe just for two hours, but it will be a passionate two hours.

If he simply hasn't yet deleted his Tinder application and his profile is not active, does that make him a treacherous villain? What about you—have you deleted yourself from the site? Or is it like your attempts to give up smoking—just one last cigarette is allowed? It's only the beginning of the relationship, so don't get carried away and don't allow yourself to control everything straight away. How do you feel—good? Enjoy the happy moments and soon you will no longer see that little pictogram on his phone. Especially as some unthinking guys amuse themselves by giving "likes" to girls on Tinder as if they were playing a video game—all while being crazy in love with you. So focus on what the two of you are sharing; don't think about the outside world, and don't listen to the gossip of ill-intentioned friends. Stay in your champagne bubble!

GOLDEN RULE:
Don't spy on him! Don't exhaust yourself with such things—it leads nowhere good. You also have a past and a secret garden and find it strangely enjoyable to chat with that handsome stranger on Facebook . . .

I messed up my sext.

"I'm in the shower, the glass is all steamed up, and I'm burning up wanting to feel you like this hot spray, running over my breasts, along my thighs, and kissing me all over like this walrus." There you go. You've put your foot in it. Dead in the water, so to speak. The killer typo. Two hours later, you've gotten dressed again and you still haven't heard from him. You can send an "Oops, I meant 'water.'" But it's too late.

Instead of thinking porn, your lover was thinking spelling mistakes . . . On top of which, on Saturday lunchtime he was still at the office/having a coffee with his sister/at an outdoor market with his niece. In short, it was a bad moment. So what? Once again, stop beating yourself up! Act as if nothing happened and continue: "Okay, I'm naked in bed and I can't stop thinking about what we'll do when you're here." He doesn't reply? Forget it and move on to something else. Be simple. There will always be time for him to reread these sexts later when he wants to. And you'd better believe it: He will want to.

GOLDEN RULE:

When you go for it, you go for it. Don't send an excessive number of sexts, but when you do, you should be shameless. Whenever you make a faux pas, think of Madame de Maintenon: She started out penniless, a semicourtesan, and the wife of an old man crippled with rheumatism, and she ended up marrying Louis XIV! The point we are making? You can go wrong in life. Start badly. Fall down. The important thing is to dare to get up again . . . and you can do it.

All we do is make love.

Is your body all he wants? You see each other only late at night, or at best late in the evening, and always at the last moment. As a result, your affair is as murky as the night that brings you together; before you know it here you are in the middle of a Count Dracula story. You only meet within four walls, while in the romantic film that keeps running in your head you have tea at the Grand Mosque and have your neck kissed in the Albert Kahn gardens.

Frankly, there is a problem. Either you have nothing to say to each other and few things in common, and so you instinctively confine yourselves to animal lust, or you're scared to make your affair real: If it exists, you can lose it, and that means suffering. In short, you want your love to be experienced in broad daylight and to set the record straight. What is the bad impulse here? To invite him to dinner—that smacks of work, a skills assessment, "I've got something to say to you." Instead, suggest forgetting nighttime for once and arrange to meet for breakfast at a café.

GOLDEN RULE:
Love in the catacombs is a catastrophe. After a month or two, it is out of the question for a relationship to remain strictly nocturnal. Be a fool for love—but not to that extent!

The main thing is to get out, have a change of scene, and make your affair into something other than *Last Tango in Paris* in a small apartment (especially if he doesn't even look much like Marlon Brando). If he refuses, refuse him: The night belongs to him but not you. Farewell, my friend!

Parisian Tip

THE CHARLES AZNAVOUR

Charles Aznavour wrote a thousand love songs, always superb even if not always hopeful, but there is one that you need to keep in mind and hum whenever you lose patience: "There is a time for spring and for sighing/A time for love, a time too for crying/A time for dreams and for sweet pretending . . ." This little trick will help you remember that a love affair is not something that runs like clockwork; you need to give it time and you need to respect the other person's time and timing (he might want in an hour what you want straight away). But not too much!

Surprise! He's married.

It happens. You never wanted to break up a family and he did not want to be seen as a jerk, but there it is—you kept running into each other every morning on the terrace of the café where you meet your girlfriends for an umpteenth coffee and you end up chatting, laughing, and exchanging numbers . . . and now, without meaning to, the two of you are in love—when he is already taken!

Look, if he's there, it's because things are not working out for him at home and it's all based (at least to some extent) on lies. We are not taking a moral or religious perspective and we don't say that because of his wife—after all, if they split up, she can find another man who will be faithful to her!—but for you. Get out of there as fast as you can! It's a hellish idea. Really, really hellish.

But then, there is Angelina Jolie. And a whole series of free women who don't give a damn what anyone thinks—whether it be the French bohemiam novelist George Sand, who, between Alfred de Musset and Franz Liszt (whom she stole from a girlfriend), had a rough time of it with a married man; Colette, who sexually initiated her own son-in-law and had already had three husbands by 1925; or Françoise Sagan, the "charming little monster" who drove in bare feet and loved both men and women—and sometimes those who belonged to other people. Literature is full of examples. It's your life, and you are a great romantic.

But here, too, you need to be careful. Say to yourself that either he leaves his marriage immediately—particularly if he doesn't have children—or within the first six months (unless you then give him six more). If not, listen to yourself and leave him. You will not live in his shadow.

GOLDEN RULE:
It's not for you to push him into leaving, it's for him to make his own decisions, knowing that you won't wait for him forever. And if it lasts? He doesn't sleep with you if he doesn't stay the whole night with you, and he should introduce you to all his friends—in short, you lead a normal life together. You are not a mistress, you are a new hope and maybe even the luckiest thing that ever happened to him (and, we hope, to you).

Should I tell him EVERYTHING?

What you tell him depends on what it is. You have different conversations with your pharmacist, your florist, and your bank manager. And you don't say the same things to your friends, your therapist, your family, and your lover.

If you want to open up about a childhood secret or a wound, we would advise waiting a bit. That's almost always better. But it's for you to judge, according to how open the two of you are generally with each other. You don't keep your clothes on in front of a naked man.

If you want to talk to him about your worries concerning work, your weight, or your girlfriends, we say: Halt! These things are love killers (for others, see the list below).

If you want to criticize him—"You could have brought flowers/warned me earlier/called me at eight like we agreed!"—we issue an even stronger "no"!

List of love killers:

- Talking about your ex
- Talking for talking's sake
- Making lists or plans about "us"
- Talking about your parents
- Talking about your embarrassing ailments (or listing all your digestive problems, unless you are with a fan of Judd Apatow movies)
- Talking about your administrative hassles (a flood, a complicated application, etc.)
- Talking about your therapist
- Talking about your work in detail
- Talking without listening
- Talking without laughing

GOLDEN RULE:

Fault-finding is ugly. Little by little, you gently find out about each other and you adapt yourselves to fit each other (like a perfectly broken-in pair of shoes!).

Should you always follow your girlfriends' advice?

Parisian Tip

THE CAFÉ REGULARS

The café regulars are those gals who have so much spirit and whom you run into often without calling them on a daily basis—from the friend of a friend who is such an astute psychologist, to that office colleague, to your sister-in-law: With them, you can talk with complete frankness and clarity. If they are anything like Parisiennes, no relationship will shock them and they will be able to view you objectively. The best idea is to talk to a guy! He's always blunt but full of good sense.

No! Why? Because your old girlfriends are like parents or siblings who always make the same jokes around the Sunday dinner table—they have known you a long time, and they still see you as if you were fourteen and talking about your first kiss. Or they have permanently filed you away in a box, a box labeled "nice," but still a box.

In any case, why ask their opinion? Unless it's to hear the advice you want? Deep down you know the few vital rules: Don't imagine yourself in someone else's head; don't fool yourself; and trust your instincts.

Your girlfriends are for everything else!

GOLDEN RULE:

Protect your relationship. It's like a baby sparrow that's fallen out of the nest, or something equally fragile. Do not talk about it with every friend and acquaintance—every response you get could unjustifiably influence you. And if you don't succeed in listening to the little voice inside yourself, there again you should hibernate and protect yourself: Find a quiet spot, if necessary quite far away from him. You must leave things to their own good time!

Things are a bit chilly this week. Is he leaving me or just taking a breather?

You are the only one who knows the status of your relationship. Deep down, you know that after an intoxicating beginning you must each return to your usual habits for a while—he to his poker friends and you under the blankets because you feel the need to be alone with a good book.

Stop worrying. Your relationship isn't like a Hollywood film? So much the better—that means it's real! Each of you just needs to withdraw for a while to have renewed energy for the game. He's distant? Give him some space, and do the same for yourself. It will do you good to rediscover your precious freedom. Or, exaggerate the good times you are having and your fun singles evenings. He will soon return to the fold.

Above all, you need to stop measuring love, like a hypochondriac constantly taking her temperature. Good moments are not weighed by the gram, like loose tea at the Parisian teashop Mariage Frères!

GOLDEN RULE:
Even if you spend a so-so evening together, you should label it a "good" evening. And say so. Add that cherry on top of the cake. The power of suggestion really works: You will begin to see a whole string of happy moments lighting up your sky, one after the other, like celebratory fairy lights.

Do you go for your opposite or your twin?

How well-matched is too much? It's a difficult question. You will be extremely bored if you share the same opinion on every subject. And extremely bored if he never understands any of your tastes or thoughts.

The solution lies between the two extremes. So he spends his grocery trips at the meat counter when you are a passionate advocate of animal protection and vegetarianism? On the other hand, like you he dreams of going to Tokyo, of visiting all the exhibitions in New York, of holding great, laughter-filled dinner parties with your combined sets of friends, of sitting anywhere beside you watching the world go by, of making love in every position and at every hour of the day during your days playing hooky. Those are the things that matter. In short, a couple that is too well-matched is like wearing the same nail polish on your hands and feet, or matching panties and bra all the time: much too predictable for you!

GOLDEN RULE:
Don't run your man down because he surprises you. His tastes do not matter—the important thing is the magical link between you. Carla Bruni loved both Mick Jagger and Nicolas Sarkozy because the feeling of love is much more beautiful and complex than a simple matter of similarity!

His best friend thinks that Paris was named after Paris Hilton.

That is what comes of kissing all and sundry! If you wanted someone who runs with an intellectual crowd, you should have gone to pick up a man at the Perrotin gallery, not at the Baron club, where everyone turns up. But the main question is: Does it matter? You are not your lover, he is also not his best friend! Let people live their lives, for heaven's sake! Take advantage of the opportunity for a little humility check, always good for the pretentious intellectual slumbering in every Parisian.

GOLDEN RULE:
You never criticize friends. Or, as we will see, family. It's idiotic and it serves no purpose. In any case, in time, as a couple you will see only people you both like.

How to go to the bathroom at his place

You are a human being and you have a digestive system. Yes. There's nothing shameful about that. Henri IV used the chamber pot in front of his subjects; you don't have to copy him, but there is no shame in going to the bathroom. Tell yourself that men couldn't give a damn. You are beautiful and self-confident enough not to put on airs and graces. Sexy but not cutesy. Look at the novel *Belle du Seigneur,* which Albert Cohen wrote precisely in order to denounce the quirks of excessive romanticism. Long story short: It finishes very, very badly. So do not put yourself on a fake pedestal. The fall always comes as a rude shock!

GOLDEN RULE:
In the event of a sexual marathon lasting a whole weekend, don't risk getting cystitis or an intestinal occlusion. If you can, go out to have a drink at a luxury hotel (they always have fantastic bathrooms, also to be used during a shopping trip), but if not, put on a film or some music and run to the bathroom at his place. Sure, you light a match in there and run water—even if it isn't ecological. But you are not embarrassed: You are a woman, not a porcelain vase, and only the latter can get by without basic bodily functions!

I think he really wants to leave me.

You haven't seen each other for a week and he hasn't contacted you for two days . . . in other words, something is amiss. Even the ultimate pleasure of nibbling a still-warm baguette as you leave the bakery seems empty. Life is terrible.

But it's out of the question for it to remain so. What do you do? First of all, you put an end to the suffering and you finish things, head high, before he does. If he was simply a bit preoccupied, he'll beg you to come back. If he acknowledges receipt without emotion, there are two possibilities: Either you go directly to the following page or you attempt to win him back. How? First, by saying clearly that you want to be with him. That's disarming! Second, by being more "Three Musketeers"—full of spirit and joie de vivre. Work like a mad thing, see your friends again, keep a tight hold of your backbone. Be the fantastic girl you are, the reason he fell in love with you in the first place—and he will fall again.

GOLDEN RULE:
Always remain prepared to withdraw to a distance again. And talk about other things with your friends, so the sadness does not spread.

Parisian Tip

KARL LAGERFELD

King Karl is surrounded by people who worship and adore him, from his ponytail to his rings, not to mention his cat, Choupette. It's because he loves himself enough to surround himself only with people who love him! Do the same thing, and say to yourself that you are far too marvelous to waste time with someone who will never be able to realize that.

THE NOUGARO CLICHÉ

Claude Nougaro sang a famous and beautiful song about desperately searching for a young girl in Paris at night because she had threatened to drown herself in the Seine, believing he did not love her. It's beautiful—but it's ugly at the same time. You don't do that, neither to yourself nor to someone else. Generally speaking, it will be truly over afterward. If you want to bring out the histrionics, be careful—that is a scene that can be played only once. If you go to the banks of the Seine, do it instead to recite these lines by Apollinaire: "Below the Mirabeau bridge flows the Seine/And our love, must I then/recall after the sorrow, joy again." It will return! You have seen it happen before!

He doesn't excite me anymore. How to end it?

"There are days when Cupid doesn't give a damn," crooned the French singer Georges Brassens—days when you lose your modesty but not your head and where love is nothing but a casual fling! You have dinner together, but the intoxication is caused more by the wine than by his fingers on yours. You make love, but it has all the effect of an abs and buttocks workout. You send each other texts that are no sooner written than forgotten. You never have knots in your stomach or a racing heart. It's lukewarm, and that's that.

So what? You can't win every time around, especially since the jackpot is you!

GOLDEN RULE:
The sooner you end it, the better. And no looking back (he risks thinking you want to get back together again and calls you more often than the bank!). Move on without revenge if he was a jerk (you don't lower yourself to his level), and without nastiness (and never by text!).

Good places to end it

Obviously, you don't end the relationship with all his friends present, just as you avoid breaking up on his birthday. Other than that, where to say to him (and it always works), "It's not you, it's me"?

You don't exactly organize a breakup as you do a proposal, but if you need a few symbolic places to deliver the coup de grâce, here is some Parisian inspiration:

THE CLIGNANCOURT FLEA MARKET
Because this affair was nothing but a cheap trinket.

MUSEE D'ORSAY
A station is romantic, especially one that has become a museum. You are leaving for good!

LE SALON DE L'AGRICULTURE
Because he was a bit of a pig.

PLACE DES VICTOIRES
Because your freedom has won out.

In the middle of LES HALLES, rue de la Truanderie, because this guy was a rip-off.

The steps of the PALAIS DE JUSTICE if you want to play it like a television series.

At metro station LA FOURCHE because you have reached a fork in the road and you are each going your own way.

At patisserie LADURÉE because its duration has ended.

On the MIRABEAU BRIDGE because love is like an ever-moving river.

SIMONE
DE BEAUVOIR
LE
DEUXIÈME
SEXE

Being single is also a blast! Or, what to do when you are heartbroken . . .

There you are: It's over. The worst thing is, it wasn't that good. But, in an unfortunate paradox, the more of a dead loss a relationship was, the more sacrifices it demanded and the worse you feel when it is over. All that for so little?

We're not going to say to you, "Plenty more fish in the sea" or suggest you go and dance to disco tunes at the Club Med in Morocco and start up a relationship with someone else. No. What you need to do is let go. Weep buckets.

GOLDEN RULE:

Really let go. Delete the texts, the photos, the name—forget his Facebook profile!—and shut yourself up with a bag of cookies, plunge into a warm bath, and listen to plenty of love songs, telling yourself that there is always someone sadder than you. If a good surprise happens and you meet someone else, you will be healed, not pathetic!

Parisian Tip

THE SIMONE VEIL

Think of all those great French women you admire. Why do you admire them? For their successful marriages? Because of how many children they have? Not at all. Some of them were unhappy in love but they were adventurers, writers, politicians, and fighters. They grabbed hold of life and defended love in other ways. So, yes, being in a couple is important, but it is far from everything. Living grandly and rebelliously like those women, with your head held high—that is truly marvelous!

THE ROMEO CLICHÉ

"It's him for me, me for him in life," sang Édith Piaf in "La Vie en Rose." Yes, but . . . that idea needs to be thrown out the window! The idea of Mr. Right, like the idea of a soulmate, is a mistake. Thank goodness! (There are several, not just one.) The one who will share part of your future will be precisely that man with whom you want to create something, not just the one who locks eyes with you in some fateful way. The man who overwhelms you with happiness will do you good for a long time—a very long time.

The five best public benches to kiss on

Find your own local versions of these romantic Parisian locations . . .

Under some bushes at the **JARDIN DES ARCHIVES**. Because it's a garden that resembles a secret passage where you can love each other beneath the singing birds, surrounded by flowers, in the heart of the Marais. "The countryside in Paris," as they say!

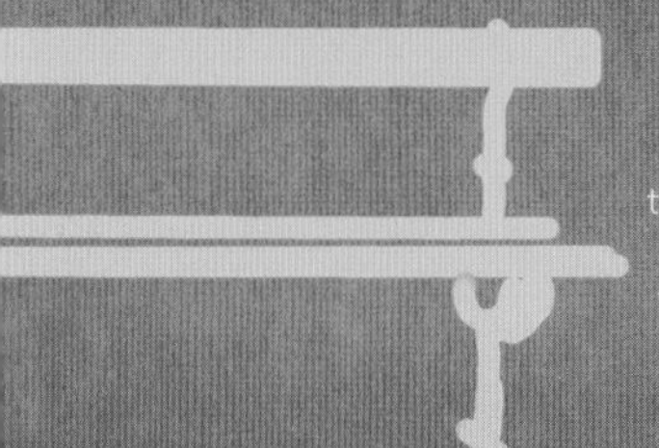

In the **JARDIN DES TUILERIES** opposite the statue by Paul Belmondo, *Apollo and Jeannette*. Because there you have your back to passersby and you tell yourself that the most beautiful man, like Apollo, can fall in love with the cute Parisienne, Jeannette. And vice versa!

A stone bench in the square courtyard of the **LOUVRE**. Because there, tourists pass by without seeing you, and opposite there's the Pont des Arts with a violinist playing underneath an archway; and because if love is making you hot, you can go and sprinkle yourself with cold water from the fountain . . . It's Rome in Paris!

In the SQUARE DU VERT GALANT. Because here you can replay the scene in *Titanic* with Leonardo DiCaprio behind Kate Winslet: It's the bow of the Île de la Cité! Here you can kiss with one of the most beautiful sunsets in the world as your backdrop.

In MONTMARTRE under the arbor of the **MARCEL BLEUSTEIN-BLANCHET** square. Because while it is true that the view from the other side is lovely, here life is beautiful: You are sheltered by drapes of Virginia creeper, hidden from people in your own dream, and free to abandon yourselves to your hearts' content!

Le Journal du Dimanche

Ick, he's too clingy! Things are moving too fast! His messages are idiotic!

You're going about your daily life when you get a text, and then another: "I miss you." "Are you okay?" "Dying to see you." "See you tonight." "Great to see you." "I adore you." And your treacherous thoughts in response? Oh, give me a break! Can't I have some space?

You are wrong. Love is magnificent and should be welcomed with open arms. If you can't do that, don't tell yourself you are looking for love. Perhaps you prefer the single life? Why not (see page 113)? But if not, consider Molière's play *The Misanthrope*, in which he explains that people who are truly in love "think their faults perfections . . . the giantess seems a very goddess in their sight; the dwarf is an epitome of all the wonders of Heaven!" Your lover, who has the exhilaration of Jacques Brel at the Olympia, the panache of a table at luxury restaurant Caviar Kaspia, the mad courage to send you sweet and affectionate messages so early on—he understands that love is rare and deserves everything. He even overlooks your faults.

GOLDEN RULE: You do not mess with love and you do not spit in the face of love. He turns you into a fool? Lucky you! It's the basis of everything, and it's fantastic.

And so you revel in that excusable adoration! This man is not dumb. He is in love!

THE CARMEN CLICHÉ

Georges Bizet's opera is one of the most beautiful in the world—but what a sad story! Carmen is stunningly lovely and a free spirit, but also destructive. At the end, everyone dies unhappy and unloved. It could have been so wonderful to sing, "I belong to you." We are not here to make each other suffer. If you love him, let yourself be loved—don't be an idiot.

He's wonderful . . . What if he's the one?

If your relationship continues and is nothing but happiness, sunshine, and joy, so that the more you see each other, the more you love each other, the desire to go away for a weekend is consuming you both, you want to introduce all your friends and your families to each other, and you declare, "I don't want to leave you for a minute"—why hold back? For sure, another, unknown life awaits you. Don't fall victim to fear of commitment.

To love is to risk. Think of all those fears you have overcome and how wonderful that was: the time you were a waitress in a seedy Miami bar, the time you went to see a German boyfriend in Dresden when you had only known him for two days, the time you first took your clothes off with someone?

And really, why would you want it to stop? Happiness is also an option, you know: Jump on him. Sing Céline Dion. Dance!

GOLDEN RULE:

Don't project into the future; don't wonder whether he will be the father of your children, or imagine yourself getting old together. Just enjoy each succeeding day.

Parisian Tip

THE PUBLIC BENCH TEST

Sit down there, on a bench. Cut yourself off from time, from the crowd, from the rat race. Just for a few minutes. Breathe. Look carefully all around you. Now, close your eyes. How are you? Do you feel a kind of warmth in the pit of your stomach and a smile coming to your lips? Yippee! It is time for Part 2.

PART 2

Encore! Encore! Still together!

You have begun a new chapter. You can't believe what's going on in your heart: It's soaring, jumping, singing with joy! Yes, it's gentle, good, and warm . . . and also terrifying! Like a good Parisienne, you fear first of all giving up your freedom. Second, more prosaically, you fear losing your head in this affair; and, third, you fear losing him!

The first year is a multitude of questions—nice ones, it's true, but still a bewildering number of them: What to do when you have your first argument? What if, one evening, you start to feel bored—is it the beginning of the end? Where to go away for the weekend without seeming like a couple of retirees on a boutique hotel trip? Should you share all your fantasies, including telling him that you sometimes want to marry him? Hang on a minute: Gently does it. In Paris, a burgeoning love affair is more than a voyage to the end of the night, more than a thousand stolen kisses—it is a life lived on the edge, a joyous revolution!

Help, he's fantastic! I'm scared I'll lose my freedom!

You are in love. And it's scary. But hold on—nobody's asking you to give up anything! What man would fall for an exuberant free spirit, a woman who jumps on him as soon as he steps out of the elevator and who comes home tipsy on rosé after an evening with girlfriends and then want her to return to the fold as some mournful, sensible, and docile creature wearing satin mule slippers?

Perhaps, passionately in love as you are, you fear that this burgeoning love affair will cause a revolution in your life. First of all, your new love is in all probability as elated—and as terrified—as you are. In that case, what could be more exciting than a new life; you're each departing for adventure and discovery of the other like a Columbus en route to America. Discovering oneself, letting oneself be discovered, is to embark on a game of strip poker with a jackpot just waiting to be won!

GOLDEN RULE:
Dare to embrace this new happiness with all the wondrous possibilities that go along with it—but always keep a good tote bag with a change of clean clothes on hand so you can get away if you need to.

Do you fear that you're packing yourself neatly away? That all thrills will be over? You are wrong. New freedoms open up to you as well as new challenges far more enthralling than worrying about whether someone will call or not. Wild holidays with ten of you? In a couple, you can always meet up with your group and get away for a few days of carefree travel. Going out? It will be as much fun as ever—with the added bonus of ending up in his bed. Your silly romantic fantasies? You are finally going to live them out: Trips on a pleasure boat are now all yours!

Who should call first? Are we still playing the game?

Falling in love is not like entering a monastery. You do not give up seduction. You remain a man and a woman who engage in an erotic dance. Think of the French classics: Once the hero in Benjamin Constant's *Adolphe* had actually conquered the woman about whom he had fantasized so intensely, she seemed to collapse like a soufflé. So, obviously, you must continue playing. Strategy is like taking your makeup off before you go to bed, going into a bookshop to feed your mind on little phrases gleaned at random, or going out on a Tuesday evening: all part of a healthy lifestyle. So you are rarely the first one to call, you don't change your Facebook status to "in a relationship," you are not always available, and you wait for him to ask for news when you go away to Copenhagen for a weekend with your girlfriends.

GOLDEN RULE: Remember our rule on page 36: Always let him be a step ahead. Old-fashioned? Yes, but it leaves him wanting more. When he calls you first, when he chases you a little, when he turns up unexpectedly and waits for you on the doorstep, it feels good. The beginnings, the middles, and even the endings are always a matter of seduction.

Parisian Tip

THE METRO TRICK

Use the "There's no reception here" tunnel trick. If you feel your desire to call is too strong, cut the contact by simply turning off your mobile phone. During the time it takes to get from Étoile to St. Paul or from Odéon to Château d'Eau, you will have calmed down and realized there is no point in trying to reassure yourself by calling him; and in any case he will probably have given in and called you!

The nightclub, the opera, or the bookstore: your first outing as a couple

Couples in love are foolish. You take pleasure in the slightest things. So follow your heart's desire! As long as it's sincere. You can't invent a passion for ballet director Maurice Béjart if you don't know who dancer Benjamin Millepied is, or take on a life as a queen of the night if you don't even know the name of the bouncer at the door of the nightclub. Instead, go back to your list of the thousands of interests, concerts, films, places, and authors to discover and tell yourself it will be even more fun to experience them with someone else.

Don't change your tastes! Go and have dinner at a famous restaurant. Walk for hours and go out until the early morning. And his pleasures? Taste them as much or as little as you feel like! It could be football Sundays or museum tours, according to the kind of creature he is.

LES SECRETS D'UNE PARISIENNE:
You love French composer Hector Berlioz? Take him to the Bastille opera before ending up at the Tuileries street fair licking your cream-covered fingers over a shared waffle!

GOLDEN RULE:
Let yourself be carried away! As in bed, each of you introduces your turn-ons to the other. But best of all is to launch into that flight of fancy to explore a third path—the one that belongs only to the two of you. You will find yourself doing things as a couple that you have never done by yourselves.

He has bizarre fantasies.

The two of you were a bit drunk coming back from dinner, steaming and ready to fall on each other on top of a car . . . when you suddenly heard him saying, "Shall we film ourselves?"

Hmm, maybe not . . . It's not so much that you have a moral position on the subject—after all, as long as nobody is hurting anyone, it's fine—but more the physical position that bothers you: You have no desire to see a video of yourself sitting astride your lover like someone possessed! Not to mention the risk that it might appear on social networks.

Whether you agree or not does not matter, but the most important thing is to tell yourself that everybody has fantasies they cannot confess. It is good your man is sharing his with you. You can confide yours—the ones that are made to be acted out, the ones that are made to excite you—and that's all. The hottest and most erotic thing about it is that you both dare to bare yourselves in that way. That is what is delightful in a relationship that endures—isn't it true that you make love better today than you did when you were eighteen? It's the same for a relationship that endures: You will go further and further, get stronger and stronger and better and better.

GOLDEN RULE:
There is no morality between consenting adults! Blossoming sexuality involves talking to each other, sharing with each other, and daring to do things. And you can say yes, just as you can say no!

Sleeping at his place—negligee or naked?

You sleep at his place for the first time not on an impulse after some adventures between the sheets but because you wanted an evening cuddling up together on the sitting room sofa watching an old movie. Obviously you are going to sleep in his arms. But how? Totally naked or in a silk negligee like Grace Kelly in *Rear Window*? She turns up at James Stewart's apartment with a tiny vanity case from which she removes an extravagant creation of pink silk and little satin mules . . .

It's up to you! You will perhaps choose to

1 Remain entirely naked
2 Put on a sexy negligee
3 Steal one of his old T-shirts
4 Keep on the shirt that you were wearing for dinner
5 Put on the shirt and shorts ensemble that you had left at his place

For those of you who replied something other than 1, 3, or 4, beware: Don't bring your vanity case or leave your overnight things as though to mark out your territory, with your hairs on the brush . . . Love is an adventure! You bring only the contents of a travel kit.

GOLDEN RULE: You can be indecent (by staying naked), dirty (by keeping on your old T-shirt), or a thief (by filching his things); but have fun—life is more exciting when you mix things up!

THE I WOKE UP LIKE THIS CLICHÉ

No, you're not perfect when you wake up! Don't get up early to go and get made up again and do your hair before slipping back nonchalantly beneath the covers. You remain, as the playwright Racine said, "beautiful, without adornment, in the simple apparel of a beauty who has just been awoken from sleep." This promises colorful mornings!

Mini makeup bag

A mini makeup bag is wonderfully multipurpose—it can be used for a quick touch-up before dinner or during an impulse weekend. If you have a large purse you can always leave your makeup bag inside; if not, keep it in your car or a drawer in your desk. The following are items that might be found in any chic Parisienne's purse:

THE BAG: You can find very attractive makeup bags at Paul & Joe Sister. The contents should include the vital (and multifunctional) minimum to look good at cocktail hour.

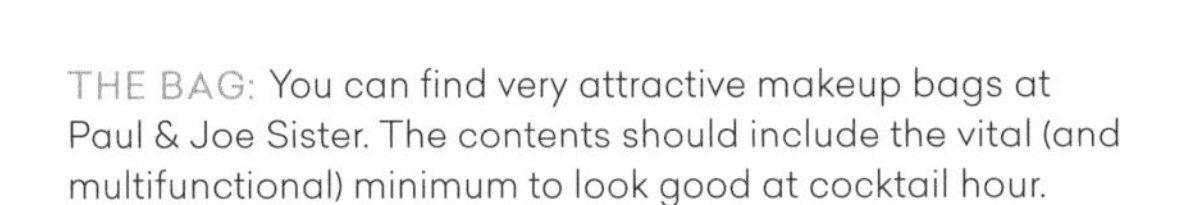

MASCARA: Eyes to Kill by Giorgio Armani.

EYELINER: Atelier du Sourcil.

HIGHLIGHTER PEN: Yves Saint Laurent Touche Éclat to conceal bags or redness, to touch up, or to put just under the eyebrow arch or the inner corner of the eye to brighten your expression.

BLUSHER: By Terry, mousse or powder, as you prefer. Or a bottle of LIQUID BLUSH—Benetint by Benefit to put on cheeks and lips for an immediate natural-looking complexion.

A TUBE OF HOMEOPLASMINE: As a lip balm, a highlighter for cheekbones, or eyeshadow to make your eyes shine.

MINI DRY SHAMPOO: Klorane. Karl Lagerfield swears by this for his white ponytail!

BEAUTY ELIXIR: Caudalie spray for an express burst of freshness on top of light makeup.

EAU DE TOILETTE: Fleur d'Oranger by Courrèges for a little touch of springtime in love.

I'm scared his children won't like me.

You haven't met them yet but you have already written out the list of your favorite childhood dishes and you're ready to serve up your best ham-and-cheese pasta shells. As elsewhere, we always come back to our golden rule: Know yourself! That will enable you to find the right distance. True, you are not their mother, but you love everything about your man, especially his little darlings who have asked for nothing. So, without overdoing it, help their father make them a dinner (keeping your aperitif glass in one hand), run them a bath (while finishing a game of Operation with them), if that takes your fancy . . . And if they say, "Ugh, you're ugly"? You don't reply, "So are you!" You remain adult and keep your sense of humor. But you respond with your own weapons: You take them to the amusement park or to the first toy store you come across to buy them something! It's base—but it works, and it gives them pleasure.

GOLDEN RULE:

You are not their mother or their best friend; but you're also not a stranger. Visualize yourself as a sympathetic aunt. If you love cooking crêpes that you then spread with Nutella, playing hide-and-seek, or organizing a great pizza evening—dive in and enjoy yourself! You have a greater than usual opportunity to return to childhood—until the babysitter arrives, along with the joy of getting back to your adult games!

I can't help it—I hate that he's a periodontist!

Your eyes sparkled when your ex told you, "I'm a photographer"—a profession that is to thirty-something women what a guitarist is to high school girls. Oh, those unforgettable portraits he was going to take of you! No, alas: He specialized in school photos. "Producer" was promising—you could really see yourself starring in his next film. Ah, but it turns out he only worked in the business sector, making commercials for a commuter rail corporation. So a periodontist, why not? What if he's responsible for George Clooney's smile? You can go to the celebrity holiday parties! In other words, you cannot take the profession at face value. A lawyer can be funny, just as a DJ can be boring!

GOLDEN RULE: Don't judge the profession, but instead take note of the approach, the involvement, the way in which your man experiences it and talks about his job. Those days spent hunched over other people's mouths is his way of playing the piano standing up and of making others happy. Or maybe just of making a good living? The last thing he needs is to be ashamed of what he does.

Parisian Tip

THE CHRISTINE LAGARDE

Do you know who the partner of the first woman president of the International Monetary Fund is? No—because you don't give a damn. A great woman does not need a man to shine. So let your beloved plunge into gogo dancing if that appeals to him. Head high and standing as tall as the Eiffel Tower, the Parisienne is far above concerns about what people would say.

My friends are his friends?

After you've been together for a month or two, there comes a time when all your friends have listened to you talking about him for long enough and they suggest, "Why don't you bring him with you?" Yes, a thousand times yes—what could be better than introducing the other into your world, to meet new future friends?

In theory, any suggestion works. But beware! Avoid the couples' dinner organized two weeks in advance, your university buddies' reunion full of in-jokes, and, obviously, your office Christmas party.

Introducing him to your friends should be an improvised affair that just happens, like love—everybody's going out for Friday happy hour and it would be so great if he joined you; a group of your friends is arranging a spontaneous karaoke evening; or you are at a friend's house party not far from where he lives, and it would be fantastic if he could drop in. Whatever happens, don't make it into a drama.

GOLDEN RULE:
Put a stop to the anxiety of "What will they think of him, of me?" You are not him and he is not you; your friends know and love you as you are, whoever you are with. The same goes for him! You have the right to be a bit shy, even distant—think of the song by Julien Clerc about how "you may not sometimes like the way she is mine but she is . . . the one I want." He might make you a bit embarrassed—he looks at himself in the mirror as he dances, he doesn't say a word and then suddenly brings out a dirty joke!—but whatever it is, you are not there to please others but to get to know each other. Above all, no final grades!

LES SECRETS D'UNE PARISIENNE:

Where to introduce him to your friends

At LA PALETTE, you all sit around with a bottle of wine and a platter of charcuterie. We love this old-fashioned bistro where Cézanne and Picasso used to come and where you now find the gilded youth of Paris.
43, rue de Seine, 75006 Paris. Tel: 01 43 26 68 15.

At the MANSART, which cultivates the same spirit but on the Right Bank, without the old café feel but with rock as a bonus.
1, rue Mansart, 75009 Paris. Tel: 01 56 92 05 99.

At the unmissable JOE ALLEN, where you can enjoy a burger on Sunday because, as a good Parisienne, you did not go out on Saturday night and are dying of hunger after an afternoon siesta.
30, rue Pierre Lescot, 75001 Paris. Tel: 01 42 36 70 13.

The trendier LE PERCHOIR for its rooftop, its cocktails, and its magnificent view overlooking Paris.
14, rue Crespin du Gast, 75011 Paris. Tel: 01 48 06 18 48.

LE WANDERLUST, on the roof of the Cité de la Mode et du Design, where the terrace is beyond all comprehension for a Parisian used to squeezing her chair between two paving stones. These structures on the banks of the Seine are perfect for having a drink set to music!
32, quai d'Austerlitz, 75013 Paris, or its neighbor le Nüba. Tel: 01 76 77 34 85.

His mom adores me!

Hallelujah! You think your maybe future mother-in-law likes you, and it's reciprocal! She makes an osso buco to die for and doesn't even try to give you the recipe; you congratulate her on her latest husband, with whom you've just spent an amusing hour in the smoking room; she talks about her work as if you were a girlfriend; and declares that "kids are great, but life with just the two of you is good too!" In short, this woman is more fun than many of your overworked friends. You are not far off inviting her to come dancing! But don't do it . . . because these days in-laws should be kept at a distance. Whether they are fantastic or unbearable, you are much too independent to worry about them. There is no need to even think about it: Spending time with his family is like Christmas week—an abundance of mouthwatering food at best, exhausting at worst, but, when all is said and done, best when occasional.

GOLDEN RULE: Never say anything bad about his mother. Pretend you really like her, even if it is not the case. At worst, you only see her at the birth of your children. At best, you invite her over for a homemade dinner of your signature couscous dish. Distance and goodwill: the perfect cocktail!

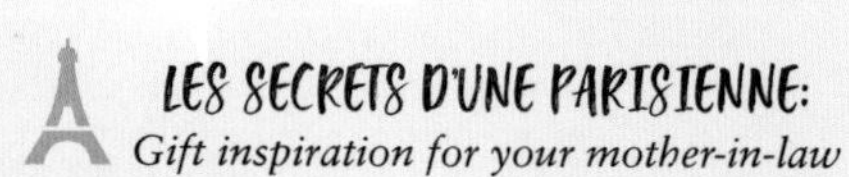

LES SECRETS D'UNE PARISIENNE:

Gift inspiration for your mother-in-law

A shawl—not the old-fashioned kind—picked out from the huge choice offered by L'ÉCLAIREUR (five locations in Paris).
www.leclaireur.com

A CÉLINE key ring.

A gift box from FRAGONARD (several stores in Paris: the one at 5, rue Boudreau, 75009, on two floors, is very impressive). You can buy classic perfumes or the black fig–Virginia tobacco super-candle or lots of little colored decorative objects.
www.fragonard.com

A DIPTYQUE candle (we like Pomander, Feu de bois, Freesia, Opoponax, Baies) or CIRE TRUDON (Odalisque, Abd El Kader) bought directly from the store at 78, rue de Seine, 75006 Paris
www.diptyqueparis.fr

A pretty notebook or a lucky charm medal to put in her bag from the chic bazaar opened by former supermodel Inès de la Fressange
24, rue due Grenelle, 75007 Paris.
www.inesdelafressange.fr

I'm so happy I'm putting on weight.

Because you're spending your weekends doing nothing but making love and emptying the refrigerator, getting up in the middle of the night to have some more goat cheese and champagne, going out to little restaurants you've discovered, and having brunches galore, you can no longer fit into your favorite jeans. Beware: If you continue to let yourself go, after a few months you'll have had it. And so you must take yourself in hand at once, but discreetly. You don't make carrot purée for the two of you, you don't threaten your man that you're going to sign him up for cellulite treatment if he has any more bread. Weight, like digestion, is an issue you keep to yourself, as is the desire to insult him when he annoys you: Going beyond that limit creates havoc! You use the stairs when the elevator is not on the first floor, and you take advantage of evenings alone to make yourself some organic soup.

GOLDEN RULE:
Being loved means being able to be the best version of yourself. Not a fat version. Not a lazy version. Not a boring version. A marvelous version! Use your desire to seduce him to stay in top form.

You have work problems, and he couldn't give a damn.

Yesterday, you suddenly couldn't bear your work any longer—it used to be great but lately has become nothing but a succession of meetings and marketing presentations. You wondered about chucking it all in to set up a bed and breakfast on the coast (as you do every three months or so).

He seemed to listen to you and adore your desire to return to nature—but then after a quarter of an hour he virtually hung up on you with, "I understand, my love, but I've got to work right now. See you tonight, okay?"

"It's disgusting," you repeat to your friends when you meet up for a cocktail. Have you chosen the wrong guy? Of course not! He is neither your father nor Father Christmas. Love has limits and that's a good thing. You are no longer a child who needs to have her tears soothed away; at this stage, it's normal that he doesn't play the part of a doting lover, there only to help you. Being present and supportive does not involve listening to the other's complaints. So don't whine, but involve him by speaking to him as a confidante, gently but with self-assurance.

GOLDEN RULE:
You are not together to be each other's crutches. He is there for you, of course, but don't ask too much too quickly. He fell for you as a strong woman who was in charge of her life.

THE BAMBI CLICHÉ

No, a girl does not have to be vulnerable to be seductive. At least not all the time. For guy things, yes; he'll fly to your aid to carry your bags or help you when you run out of gas, but for the rest, the "human being things," he will like nothing better than seeing you standing up firmly on your own two feet!

Now he complains all the time.

He's got problems? Welcome to the club! It is not your job to reassure him all the time, to cheer him up when he's sad, to fill his silences, to take him out, to feel sorry for him, or to play at being caretaker. He is not asking you for that. Yes, you are there if he needs you, but what he needs above all is to dive with you into a bubble of joy, a world in which his worries have not monopolized his heart. So let him moan; listen to him (a little), but do not put yourself in his place too much. Empathizing with him all the time brings down the mood, turns the knife in the wound, makes it seem as if you are his mother, and, to put it in a nutshell, kills love! So stop! If he has to think of you as a nurse, it is not for a thermometer but for what is under the white uniform.

GOLDEN RULE:
Stop imagining what he is thinking about or what he is feeling. His problems are often less serious than he thinks; explain that to him, gently. And if he gets on your nerves, tell him!

Rather than listening to his complaints, introduce the issue yourself in a peaceful moment when you can have a real discussion about his worries (which are, like yours, important to share).

THE NURSES ARE SEXY CLICHÉ

When you put yourself in someone else's shoes, it is not as altruistic as it seems. Really, it means you are finding an excuse for the fact that this man is less present, less funny, and more boring. Now, there isn't necessarily a real reason for this bleak period; it might just be temporary. If not, look at things head-on: If he's already an old grouch who never calls you, time to move on.

Should we go on a weekend getaway?

A lovers' weekend getaway—oh, yes! Just to be by yourselves for two whole days and nights, walking on the sand like they do in *A Man and a Woman* by Claude Lelouch, running toward each other to fall into each other's arms, making love in a romantic hotel room, eating oysters beside the waves, and coming back drunk, clinched in a tight embrace beneath the stars with a runny nose because of the evening chill by the ocean—but so in love that you couldn't give a damn.

That's his dream too! But here's the thing: A lovers' weekend is sometimes the beginning of the end. Those forty-eight hours are also a test. Staring into the whites of each other's eyes across a candlelit table in a cozy beachside restaurant with dated décor can be a magical experience—but it can also descend into disaster.

GOLDEN RULE:
The first time you go away together, make sure you have a Plan B. Choose a place where you are certain of being able to see friends. It is so good, after a long, languorous nap, to be able to go and display your happiness with your local friends. It's a foretaste of holidays to come and gives an edge of reality to your waking dream.

THE ST.-TROPEZ-IN-THE-LOW-SEASON CLICHÉ

Oh, St. Tropez in February. Like in the days of Brigitte Bardot: sunny alleyways without onlookers, the blue sea without yachts, the cries of seagulls, and none of those of sleazy women at the Caves du Roy nightclub—paradise! But St. Tropez without tourists, when you already feel nervous about finding yourself alone with your man, is guaranteed anxiety, like being at a fairground after a deadly virus that has ravaged the human population. Not good. Even the stunning Brigitte, holed up in a little shepherd's hut with the bewitching Jean-Louis Trintignant after the shooting of *And God Created Woman* by Roger Vadim, became so thoroughly bored that she got out of there pronto and ended their relationship. New relationships need animation and life. So beware out-of-season vacations that smack of retirees—not very promising in terms of sexual performance.

He's going to live in London—is it over?

Your man is leaving to work in London. He will experience sports cars, restaurants that cost an arm and a leg, and those oh-so-kitschy taxis! You too like the idea of strolling through Notting Hill, the parties that start at five in the afternoon, the girls in miniskirts when it's below freezing outside, the little parks everywhere, and above all the English accent! Yes, but. Just for a weekend. Your home is your friends, your work, happiness at your fingertips when you pass by your favorite florist or a good cheese shop. It's dinner at your favorite hole-in-the-wall spot without a reservation. It's the Sunday paper! And to continue with the clichés, you also have this one in your mind: Long-distance love never works.

Wrong! Yes, of course, loving someone means sharing a life together that is enriched by daily routine. But if it's for several months (not more—after that, you must think about migrating) turn this setback to your advantage. You will become the stranger on the *Orient Express*. So have phone sex to your heart's content and meet up for hot weekends under the British rain.

GOLDEN RULE:
Don't introduce strict rules along the lines of "We'll call each other at 8 p.m. every evening!" Abroad, everyone is in their own bubble, their own time; and you're sure to catch him at a bad moment. Instead, call when you feel like it, go visit when you choose to—that's what credit card points are for!

He's really wonderful! I'm terrified we'll split up.

You really like this guy! You love that he calls for no reason, the way he holds you tight, those dinners spent laughing with the people at the next table, those afternoons spent walking hand in hand in ecstasy as the sun sets, those jaunts in a taxi while you gaze at each other beneath the glimmering streetlights that seem to be lit up for you alone. If that ended, there'd be an enormous void.

But you're not there yet; so don't panic. You are just suffering from what is known as *happiness vertigo*. So, as though you're on a precipice or the top of the Eiffel Tower, just take a step back: Cling on to your life! Work, go out, cultivate your many friendships, and invest time in the things you are curious about. By remaining centered in your own space, you cease (for a time) to think only of him. You get your balance back, along with the joy of knowing he is there. Surely you won't fear happiness when it shows up? Above all, keep the good country-folk wisdom of our ancestors: When the crop is ripe for harvesting, you celebrate!

GOLDEN RULE: Don't let your lover sense you are scared he will leave. And learn how to make that fear something familiar that you tame, something that concerns nobody but you. Speak to your fear, tell it to leave you in peace while being grateful for its presence. Deep down, that little worry that everything will stop, is one of the secrets of love.

THE JULIO IGLESIAS CLICHÉ

God knows we love that Spaniard who has never changed, as well as his son Enrique with his gleaming shirtless torso, who whispers "Te quiero" until you're ready to swoon . . . but in reality, declarations of eternal love can scare the living daylights out of people! "Until the end of time" makes us want to hightail it without further ado. So take heart and dispense with these ritual formulas that are designed only to reassure ourselves! When someone says, "I have never felt this, I have never loved like this," it sets the bar too high—and bars, as we know, put love in a cage!

Should we talk during sex?

Parisian Tip

THE MADAME CLAUDE

Although you adore him—his hands, his skin, and everything about him—you can't seem to climb up to the very top, to the most beautiful place of all: put bluntly, to where you get your rocks off. So, make your way to a hotel! And give him a night of role-playing—both for you, one of Madame Claude's girls, the famous queen of Parisian escorts, and for him, a head of state or a young plumber, according to your tastes. Yes, we want to be respected in life, we want "More champagne, my love?" and "You're not too cold? What would you like?" In bed, however, it's the exact opposite: People want to be savage. Pretend to be that mysterious lady of the night, and ascend to seventh heaven with him!

To talk or not to talk in bed. Yes, men like women to know how to make them climax with words. And he continually whispers naughty sweet nothings in your ear that make you crazy. You are tempted to return the favor—but how? You're scared of falling into bawdiness with phrases that sound bargain-basement: "I can feel it deep inside" or, worse, a karaoke performance of a slightly risqué pop song. So go gently, like a first kiss or a first caress. You didn't leap on each other straight away in the elevator; you didn't immediately start touching in the movie theater, but brushed against each other first. It's the same thing with words: Who goes slowly, goes safely!

GOLDEN RULE:

Don't force anything! That rings false and ruins everything: No "I can really feel it, your wooden c***." It's all a matter of dosage. Begin gently by using and abusing the fail-safe, "Yes, that's good!" and other admiring declarations whispered burningly in his ear. "No, now, come on!" The rest will come as you warm up . . .

List of things we think are sexy but in fact aren't at all

SOAKING YOURSELF IN A FULL BOTTLE OF HEADY PERFUME: This makes you into a cross between an elderly courtesan and a young prostitute.

RED MOUTH, MADE-UP EYES: A combination to avoid. Choose one or the other, not both.

THE TOTAL LEOPARD LOOK: Like all total looks, this is very difficult to pull off successfully.

BARE BREASTS ON VACATION: Very hot in 1984, very uncool today.

LIP GLOSS: It sticks.

KILLER HEELS: Out of proportion when you are short, often excessive when you are tall, and obviously forbidden with a miniskirt.

HAVING COFFEE INSTEAD OF DESSERT: If you love food, go for it—order the chocolate fondant!

THE NAKED SELFIE: Hyper difficult to pull off if you're not a Kim Kardashian type who can redo the pose a thousand times to get both background and foreground right.

SHIMMER BODY OIL: Makes you look like a disco ball.

And those we think are unsexy—but in fact aren't at all!

LICKING YOUR FINGERS covered in mayonnaise/chicken sauce/Chantilly cream. Loving food is not a sin!

EATING A BIG MEAL worthy of a trucker (sweetbread, grilled andouillette sausage) or an enormous dessert. A woman who owns her appetite—that's sexy!

BEING A BIT SHY or, the opposite, a bit over the top, laughing hysterically. What could be more flattering to him than seeing the effect he has on you?

WEARING EVERYDAY UNDERWEAR. And so? You weren't expecting to make love, but he made you feverish with desire. (You mustn't use this one too often though!).

DARING TO WALK THROUGH THE APARTMENT TOTALLY NAKED, even if you aren't exactly fashion model Gisele Bündchen. Very simply, a totally naked woman is beautiful. (Think of the statues in Paris's Tuileries if you need convincing—even the sculptures of women by Maillol, with their big buttocks and small breasts, are magnificent!)

What if I'm not very good in bed?

Parisian Tip

PARIS, CITY OF LIGHTS

To really be sure you are letting go, follow the example of the City of Lights. Even its least attractive alleyways are always lit up; and you keep a light on in the room. That way, you are forced to let yourself go—and you send the signal to him (and yourself!) that you are comfortable in your skin. What could be sexier?

At the very beginning, sex is usually either really awful or fantastic. After several months, each of you knows more or less the other's go-to positions in bed. And that is when a little worry sets in. You're freaking out about things becoming too predictable. It's normal. Intoxication gives way to the beginning of routine and you are scared that your celebrated reverse cowgirl (you on top of him but with your back to him) no longer does it for him.

Don't panic! First of all, a good lay, a truly good one, is someone who likes making love. Period. You couldn't give a damn about breaking the living-room vase, catching your thigh on the corner of the washing machine, or waking the neighbors (unless, of course, it's your mother). Other than that, you can rest assured it is not up to you alone but to the two of you—your skin, your bodies, your fingers, your brains, the trust you each inspire in the other. But remember, you are not there to play Barbarella, a character open to any experience no matter how crazy, or the naïve and blushing Cécile de Volanges from *Dangerous Liaisons*. Do what you know how to do well. Sex, as we know, does not fear repetition.

GOLDEN RULE:

Help yourself to him, and come back for more. You are there to do yourself good, that's all it comes down to. The more you receive, the more you give!

Some evenings are not a blast.

You are a little bored. Usually, there are jokes, laughter, and kisses, and you talk about anything and everything—all a pretext for having fun, for gazing at each other with enchantment, and for kissing. Even a Tuesday evening at the supermarket is Broadway! But this evening, you are disagreeing about nuclear energy, he is talking about his digestion of gluten, and there are endless silences . . . And after you've made love on the bed like a married couple, after a film and before going to sleep, you find yourself wondering if a failed evening is the beginning of the end.

Of course not! It's the beginning of another story, one in which you don't need to make a fuss about things and in which both of you finally accept being yourselves. There are slumps in life; not every evening is a can-can show! If he is the man for you, he will not even pay it any attention. You don't judge each other for it.

GOLDEN RULE:
Don't twist the knife in the wound. No "So, you're not saying anything?" or "So, what are you thinking about?" Instead, read a book in a corner or plunge into a warm bath. Be like a cat: there, but not altogether; independent but affectionate. Loving is not (just) leaping on each other; it's also wanting to do nothing together . And that is fantastic.

Parisian Tip

THE NEWSPAPER CAFÉ

You both sit at an outdoor café. You order a coffee and an espresso, each get out your bundle of newspapers, watch the passersby, and enjoy the silence that falls over you. If you are happy, like two kids playing with their toys who don't need to talk, it means things are going really well between you.

He's taking me skiing . . . and I don't know how!

You really look the part: a cute ski suit borrowed from a girlfriend who is a snowboard champion, the latest sunglasses on your nose, and even triple-layer silk gloves. Fantastic, you finally have an opportunity to get out that Russian fur hat you bought in St. Petersburg. The snag? Your last memories of skiing were of the elementary-school skiing trip. You didn't even make it past the kindergarten class. How can you avoid embarrassing him in front of all his friends, who have suddenly turned into mountain men? By not being in any way embarrassed yourself! Okay, you don't know how to ski (though you do other things very well), but you will try a bit, gently . . . After the first two days spent alone with a very handsome ski instructor, you join your man on the slopes to give him the opportunity to impress you and to bombard him with cries of "Hey, what style, what a fantastic turn!" when he sways downhill beside you. Then you can let go of the ski poles and relax on the terrace of a café in the sunshine with a good glass of mulled wine. You're tipsy? A good excuse for retreating to your nest.

GOLDEN RULE:
Don't lie! Don't pretend you're a champion skier any more than that you have a philosophy doctorate. With all your good qualities, no need to invent some!

575 9 RFT 75

We always go out with friends. When do we get to see each other alone?

Be thankful you have a busy social life! Most couples quickly descend into the Facebook phase: sitting indoors, on the living-room sofa, looking at other people's lives. Your man has, like you, kept his taste for evenings out? Hallelujah! But if you are scared of becoming a couple mainly for others and barely at all for yourselves, if you feel like you are permanently living on stage and you no longer manage to spend an evening in with just the two of you, a good film, and a slice of lemon cake, take things in hand. Love is like a great opera—duets make it really beautiful!

The solution: Organize a weekend alone, no matter where. Or, even better, instead of going to that group dinner, keep driving until you get to the nearest cute little town! If moments alone are exciting getaways and not a duty, he will soon become addicted to them.

GOLDEN RULE: Don't launch into great explanations of why you aren't happy—take control and plan your own private fun. It's much more effective.

Where to go for impulse weekends away

Use the following as inspiration to plan your own romantic escape!

FROM THE PORTE D'AUTEUIL: A weekend right out of the 1960s classic *A Man and a Woman.*

Destination **CABOURG** in Normandy and its unmissable Grand Hôtel, where Proust stayed. You can eat oysters for breakfast, walk on the beach, and place bets (against a security deposit) in the casino.

You can even escape to dine at Les Vapeurs restaurant in **TROUVILLE**.

Luxury-loving bums? You can stop at the **TRIANON PALACE** in Versailles to play Marie Antoinette!

FROM THE PORTE DE BERCY: A Cinderella weekend. Sleep at the **DISNEYLAND HOTEL**, the main hotel in the theme park—not a speck of glamour in sight but lots of kitsch and five stars. You may stay only one night because kids are screaming on every side, but then you can go to Walt Disney Studios to visit Hollywood in Paris! Go back to childhood for a moment in the theme park—after all, it was here that Nicolas Sarkozy was first photographed with Carla Bruni and their relationship became official!

FROM THE PORTE D'ITALIE: An Impressionist weekend.

Destination **BARBIZON**, the painters' village (it housed Corot and Monet) situated on the edge of the Fontainebleau forest. Sleep in the Pléiades, near exquisite restaurants.

If you feel like kissing in the fields, go to **LE PERCHE** and the medieval city of Mortagne-au-Perche, an adorable little town popular with Sonia Rykiel and Chantal Thomass.

FROM THE PORTE DE LA CHAPELLE: A luxury weekend, calm and voluptous (unless you decide to have a Chantilly cream battle).

Destination **CHANTILLY** and the Tiara Château Hôtel Mont Royal. A five-star château nestling high up in the forest of Halatte. With its neoclassical architecture, the château has many exceptional features such as its front steps bordered by columns, its main courtyard, and its ballroom converted into a restaurant. In the rooms and suites, the décor is toile de Jouy, velvet sofas, and Louis XV– and Louis XVI–style furniture. To continue the royalty theme, you can visit the famous château at Chantilly or its Great Stables, built for the Prince of Condé.

I want to have his child.

It's as though you have gone back to being a child with him—everything is wonder, laughter, and play. It's the country fairground, fresh-picked strawberries, trips on rental bikes through the park. And then a couple with a baby goes by, and you surprise yourself by suddenly wanting a bit of him and you combined—in other words, a child.

Okay. If you've known each other three months, do something that will bring you back to your senses: Go to the birthday party of a friend's son where fifteen four-year-olds dressed as Spiderman are violently destroying a piñata of fluorescent candy. Have you calmed down now?

On the other hand, if you think this is it, you're really here to stay and you are really sure he's the one and this is the time . . . say nothing! When the opportunity arises, put a child in his arms (there must be one you can look after for an afternoon somewhere or other). If his heart melts and he is not embarrassed when you laughingly mention it, be bold enough to try the very cunning, "What if we made a baby? I'd love to see a tiny you."

GOLDEN RULE:

You don't have a child for social reasons. Or to be like your friends, who repeat, "Go on, it's the best adventure there is!" or because of age ("I'm nearly forty") or for any other reason at all: "I'm dreaming of being a mom," "We've been together for two years," "That way I will have checked all the boxes," or "Aren't we getting bored?" There is only one valid reason: love!

Do I confess everything?

You were out with girlfriends when your eyes met those of a handsome stranger. Then you brushed against his shoulder at the bar. When he grabbed hold of your waist, you succumbed—and your tongue suddenly found itself in his mouth as his hands explored your body. You immediately came to your senses, of course, and ran out of the nightclub as he stood in the street shouting your name into the night. Is it serious? And should you be honest and confess this misdemeanor to your beloved to preserve the purity of this burgeoning and so beautiful romance?

GOLDEN RULE:
Only kiss a stranger if he's a sex bomb and never go further than that. If you do it too often, you should leave this man to become single again. Apparently Joséphine de Beauharnais cheated on Napoleon all the time and . . . well, it's gross.

No, of course not, you idiot! What does it matter; think like a Parisian—everybody kisses in Paris! Just bury your little mistake. Don't say a thing! Forget it at once and pretend it happened before you met, that it doesn't count. Sometimes, at the beginning of a relationship, you don't always understand straight away what is happening and you don't yet act as if you are a couple—you still act as you did before, with that old Pavlovian reaction to steal a kiss from every handsome hunk who crosses your path.

I'm afraid he'll change me into someone else.

Parisian Tip

THE EMPTY FRIDGE

Or almost empty. That and a scooter (or a membership in an electric-car-sharing service) and you are sure of keeping your bohemian life: going everywhere on a whim, and having to improvise a new evening out every day.

Every relationship changes you. Despite yourself, and to the great amusement of your friends, you will find yourself at an experimental jazz concert, or walking beside the river on Sundays, or perhaps even refinishing an old armchair that you picked up together in a flea market. The beginning of a relationship can feel like retiring before you've had your youth. Or, at the opposite extreme, you may show up at a rave party at nine o'clock in the morning, go away for the weekend in a carpool (when you are dreaming only of sharing a plane), and buying the latest Doc Martens Graffiti boots.

Don't worry, things will gradually settle down. If you love this man, you will love what you become together—the fantastic combination of your desires, your friends, your fantasies, and your worlds is a delicious cocktail called the Adventure of Love.

GOLDEN RULE: Accept that you don't necessarily have the same tastes. Don't give anything up, but instead cultivate three gardens: his, your own, and the communal plot.

We've had our first argument. Is it serious?

You took a supposed shortcut that sent you straight into a rush-hour traffic jam, he laughed too much with a little floozy who was passing through, you forgot to pick up the train tickets for the weekend escape—and there you go, the tone rises, and you contemplate slamming the door or throwing a book across the room. Fantastic! But you stop yourself because violence breeds violence, and it's better to go take a walk around the block than to become hysterical.

You need to know how to argue. As Anouilh said in *Antigone*, "Happiness is full of arguments." A relationship without ripples may be a bad sign—it may mean that one of you is negating himself or herself . . . and that will inevitably break down one day. So, bravo on this heated moment! This argument is a new step—and that's what love is. All creation is based on a big bang! But arguing is also an art. Insults are forbidden, and you don't bring anything personal or below-the-belt into it. That only soils things. At the most, you steal the words Jean-Paul Belmondo launched at Jean Seberg in the French film *À bout de souffle*: "You are really disgusting." No more than that!

GOLDEN RULE:
Never threaten! Don't say, "If you continue, I'm getting out of the car," unless you are prepared to actually get out. If possible, you take the first step toward reconciliation—that's really nice. You can put your pride to one side and talk about it afterward. Much better to joke, "What idiots we are!" than try to get to sleep with tears in your eyes.

THE BRIGITTE-BARDOT-IN-*CONTEMPT* CLICHÉ

She might have been smoldering with her sulky pouts and her raven wig, but don't copy moody Brigitte Bardot in Godard's film *Contempt*. Five minutes, okay—no longer. Life is too short, and you have better things to do.

Shall I call an ex to make him jealous?

Oh, no—that is a really dumb trick! True, Odette in Proust's *Swann's Way* manages to make that great seducer Charles Swann jealous and thereby gets him to marry her. But once he has calmed down and his passion is over, Swann quickly realizes that Odette is a silly featherbrain who is, like most foolish people, cruel and "not his type." All that to say that we don't need to serve up Proust on a plate for you to understand that nothing is more idiotic than involving an ex.

An ex is not even a madeleine—to continue the Proustian metaphor—but a rancid shepherd's pie made with yesterday's leftovers. You've already tasted it and you stopped wanting to eat it long ago. It lacks style and romanticism, and you have no more need of an old lump of coal to relight the flame.

Choose a stranger on a bus instead! The handsome hunk with whom you went into fits of laughter in front of a bizarre graffiti mural. Or even the good old waiter at whom you flash your biggest smile. Let your charm radiate and say nothing: All those waves of seduction will make you so attractive, he will be cut to the quick.

GOLDEN RULE:
Never let him think that everything has been acquired, either from his side or yours. If you let people approach you just for the pleasure and without taking things further, he will have no need to be jealous—or sad or angry, which would be a shame—but will just be fascinated by you, like everyone else. That's better!

It feels like it's ending.

Nothing particular has gone wrong, but a certain weariness and sadness gradually set in. You wander through the streets hoping that Apollinaire was right and that joy always comes after pain. No. And yet you love this guy. What to do?

First of all, walk, so you can think about things. Socrates believed only in ideas that work. We do too!

And then you withdraw from the beloved (if you always keep a toe outside the relationship, this time it's a leg, right up to the thigh—shamelessly!). Either he will then show signs of returning or he won't, in which case you go on to the penultimate stage, the new love affair—with yourself! That's right. Buy yourself some gifts, take yourself to the spa, devise a glamorous getaway for yourself, spend too much, and go crazy over yourself! That way, if he hasn't come back, you will be all set for the next love affair! (For how to leave him, see page 64.)

GOLDEN RULE:
Don't fight as though this were the battle of Waterloo. In life, things sometimes don't work out, and that's the way it is. You are not Napoleon, obstinately determined to win every battle. Such people end up alone. Your combat consists of being emperor of yourself! Soldier on calmly: destination happiness!

LES SECRETS D'UNE PARISIENNE:
You take up position in the Place des Victoires—a prophetic address—and you walk around it. Then you go a bit farther to the café in the Place des Petits Pères and jot down reasons why you should stay and why you should go. You are too romantic to put up with a rocky relationship, too free to accept suffering—ground zero in terms of emotions of love—and too beautiful to give yourself to someone who does not appreciate you.

THE SPLITTING-UP-SO-AS-TO-MAKE-UP CLICHÉ

Playing at hurting yourself while hoping to do yourself good spoils love. And when it rings false, it doesn't work. So if you split up, you split up—you delete his messages, his photos, and his number, and you talk about him as little as possible. Radical measures.

LES SECRETS D'UNE PARISIENNE:

Places to cry

In the warmth of YOUR HOME. With everything that gives you pleasure: chocolate mousse, a bath, singer Patrick Bruel, and even lollipops.

At the CHAMPOLLION MOVIE THEATER. From noon on, you can hide yourself in a dark room, devouring a great film to help you forget your sadness . . . and meet a hot student from the nearby Sorbonne!

On a BENCH IN THE TUILERIES. Opposite the *Vowel Tree*, the sculpture of an uprooted tree by Giuseppe Penone in memory of the storm of 1999. "A reflection on the fragility of things," in the great sculptor's words. Then go to the Orsay Museum or to the nearby Louvre to see beauty, which is what lasts longest.

At a CLASSICAL CONCERT in the Salle Cortot, because music softens the heart.

At the MUSEUM OF ROMANTIC LIFE. With several rooms dedicated to George Sand, that free, adventurous woman, this is a place for poets and pianists in love. Make a beeline for that bench on the right under the trees at the end of the little courtyard, where you can think of all the other lovers who have wept in Paris in addition to you.

In the JARDIN DES PLANTES in front of poor Nénette, the most famous orangutan in Paris, whose life, at forty-five years old and despite her new cage, also can't be a barrel of fun. How about telling yourself there are causes bigger than humans—like that of animals!

In the GARDEN OF THE ÉCOLE NORMALE SUPÉRIEURE in the rue d'Ulm, because among the successors of Bergson, Bourdieu, Derrida, and Blum, there must be a guy who will find the right words to cheer you up!

At GIBERT JOSEPH, because it was there, at the corner of Boulevard St. Michel, that Verlaine and Rimbaud met. And because you find intelligent things to read there—on top of which, you can be seriously hit on amid the bookshelves.

At the ARÈNES DE LUTÈCE, because it put things in perspective to see retirees playing pétanque in the place where, two thousand years ago, gladiators fought to the death. Time sorts everything out!

Should you show you're jealous?

Parisian Tip

THE SIMONE SIGNORET

When Yves Montand cheated on Simone Signoret with Marilyn Monroe, what did the beautiful Simone do? She went to nab an Oscar in Hollywood and amazed everyone by saying, "If Marilyn is in love with my husband, it proves she has good taste," and, "Do you know who could resist if they took Marilyn Monroe into their arms?" We say bravo for that spirit, but we are no longer in the '50s and so we recommend keeping only the "Yes, she's pretty," which implies that nobody can rival you or your magnificent love story.

You were still trying to recall where you had parked your car when you caught him a long way behind you, frenetically exchanging text messages like a teenager. Oops. You suddenly remember the trashy woman who came on to him at a friend's dinner party the previous week.

You feel like taking his telephone, reading all his messages, telling him how ugly this girl is, and then, once you find your car, running him down.

However, you don't do any of that. Instead, you behave like a Parisian woman. For the Parisienne has style, the Parisienne is not where you expect her to be, the Parisienne is surprising! She relies on humor and throws out an "Are you sexting, darling?"—which, now that it's not secret anymore, cuts off all desire.

Above all, you don't run anyone down and you don't even interest yourself in this mysterious correspondent. Nor in him, for that matter—if he's cheating on you, he can go elsewhere; he doesn't deserve your attention. As long as you don't have proof, trust him. And, most important, reassert your own worth. More than ever, this is the moment to protect your relationship, erecting fortifications like the good old city walls built by Louis Philippe around the center of Paris. You smooch, you murmur words of love, you remember that what you have is rare and beautiful.

GOLDEN RULE:
Never show that you doubt him. Your doubt alone will make him think the thing is possible. (People are sometimes perverse.)

Since I've been in a relationship, I've felt ugly.

When you went out, you always had a sparkle in your eyes and a catch line in your head: "I'm waiting for love." You walked with a swing, jostling passersby out of the way, wearing a sexy outfit—because you never knew, love might be waiting around the corner . . .

Now, the prince is here. Beside you. Too hot for words but so in love that you know that even if you were wearing a bag he would eat you up. And you no longer wear anything but sweaters that are, like his arms, big and warm. Will you be living in a track suit in another month?

No! Because like a good Parisienne, you know that a week without attracting the attention of someone other than your man is the tip of the iceberg that sank the *Titanic*. The solution? Going out without him, after putting on a blouse that you leave largely unbuttoned and a pair of crazy shoes that electrify you. Do it to remember who you are and tell yourself it would be a shame not to be that anymore. Afterward, at each dinner with or without him, you will remember the effect you can have and will want these fireworks for him and for you!

GOLDEN RULE:
You aren't beautiful in order to be seduced, you are beautiful because nature made you that way! So celebrate nature's handiwork with a little bit of blush and a dress that hugs you in all the right places! It is a thousand times more chic to be elegant for the sake of elegance—like all the old ladies of Paris who put on their Sunday best before going to buy bread—rather than just so someone can grab you in a corner! Get a hold of yourself: celebrate the female form like a Parisienne!

We've separated. Should I go back?

Do you know how gourmets tell the difference between a good restaurant and a greasy spoon? They taste the bread. If it is crispy and crusty—basically, as if it just came out of the oven—all is well, and they place an order. If it is soft or all hard, they don't even glance at the menu.

Well, it's the same with love! You haven't had any news from that ex for months and now he's inviting you to dinner? Go, but keep a sharp eye on that bread. Does he seem to have changed? Does he seem all fresh and crusty? Or is he soft and lazy, calling you because he is alone, or hard and vengeful, contacting you because he is sad?

Whatever happens, if you start seeing him again, the relationship should be like the loaf of bread: fresh and new! Reread the whole of Part 1, don't say "yes"on the first evening, and don't flood him with texts proclaiming, "I'm over the moon!" but instead go into things as fresh as a rose in the morning dew, without dusty grudges or unrealistic hopes.

GOLDEN RULE:
Don't go back to an ex unless you have had a new life since you split up. Other lovers. Other adventures. Even another job. In short, don't go back to square one like you do when you lose at Chutes and Ladders.

SAINT GENEVIÈVE: When everyone wanted to flee from Attila the Hun (yes, him!), she entreated the women to remain. And she saved Paris.

JOAN OF ARC: A virgin and proud of it. She gave her life to kick the English out of France and was wounded in the heat of the battle to liberate Paris, at the site that is today 161, rue St. Honoré.

NINON DE LENCLOS: Because she was a courtesan who had a non-stop stream of lovers, kept them as friends, and was even admired by Louis XIV for her witticisms!

COCO CHANEL: Christened Gabrielle Bonheur Chanel, she insisted on being called "Mademoiselle." A woman with a light heart and an unchained genius!

MARIE MARVINGT: Nicknamed "the most courageous woman since Joan of Arc" and "the bride of danger." Aviator, mountain-climber, first female participant in the Tour de France bike race. In 1914 she disguised herself as a man and served on the front lines of WWI as a foot soldier, until her identity was revealed and she was sent home. She died in 1963 at the age of eighty-eight, shortly after taking a supersonic flight. Childless but with many memories.

SIMONE WEIL: The towering philosopher, author of *Gravity and Grace* and essays on social oppression. A graduate of the École Normale Supérieure, she worked as a manual laborer to get a better understanding of hardships in the workplace. A resistance fighter, she died in 1943.

FRANÇOISE SAGAN: She didn't stay married for long. Her life was her friends, casinos, books, and driving with bare feet to Normandy!

VANESSA PARADIS: She, too, was not Joan of Arc, but after she split up with Johnny Depp, she assumed her single status fiendishly well by displaying her buttocks on the front cover of *Vogue*!

He's still close with his ex-wife.

Your man and his ex-wife are still friends. They see each other every morning when he picks the children up to take them to school, and she calls him every evening when she has problems at work, problems with the kids, or when her car breaks down on the highway. Obviously he listens, is attentive, and cannot do enough for her. He's a good guy. And yet it makes your blood boil!

How to manage the situation? By understanding her for what she is: not a rival—he would not have left her if he still loved her—but as the type who will demand things to make people feel guilty: "I land at the airport on Saturday afternoon and there's nobody to pick me up!" Um, no. That is not his job anymore!

The solution? Let her be a bundle of worries, anxieties, and problems. You embody the other side—what is funny, light, independent, and seductive. And why not sometimes be nice (kindness is blind to faults!): She loses her keys, you know a fantastic locksmith; she's looking for a job, you pass on her résumé; she's looking for a guy, you are almost ready to pay for an escort boy for her. After all, even if her problems are not yours, her happiness means your man can breathe a little easier.

GOLDEN RULE: Never jealous, never dramatic, but firm. Your man is the father of her children, not her therapist. So no daily forty-five-minute telephone sessions, and no debriefing with you afterward.

His politics are different!

Everything in Paris is political, even love. So if your guy wants to vote for a candidate you find loathsome, it does not make you feel much like going to bill and coo with him in the voting booth. And since he came out with his political allegiance you have been arguing about the big issues—the minimum wage, private schools, taxes, and the latest right-wing candidate—but also about every little choice: a classic Bordeaux versus organic wine, action films or arty films, documentaries or popular TV, a weekend in the mountains or by the beach . . .

GOLDEN RULE:
Believe in your guy, like Carla Bruni believes in Nicolas Sarkozy, even though she didn't share his political views to begin with. If his opinions are different from yours, since he's a good man and you love him, it means there must be some sense in what he says.

You know what? None of it matters! It's good to bump up against the other person's views, even if only to hone your own. And it's an opportunity to admire the intelligence of this guy who, in this duel, is a hell of a fighter!

That said, if you really dream of national union in the house, you need to have at least two or three desires in common. Keep the best: You love his amusing Catholic cousin who wears her heart on her sleeve, willing to march in support of gay marriage; while he loves your antiglobalist pal who militates against the airport for ecological reasons from on board his parents' private jet. You will find plenty of material to keep things interesting!

I want to surprise him by waiting naked on the piano . . .

You've got a crazy romantic idea and you should do it! It's fantastic if the idea just comes to you on the spur of the moment when he buzzes the intercom, much the way you might feel like having a chocolate mousse, or letting your napkin drop to the floor to give him a blow job right in the middle of dinner, or taking him to the opera on a whim, or going out without a bag and without a bra—in short, a breath of freedom, sheer lunacy, and frivolity!

But think again if you intend to plan it, to rehearse dance routines worthy of a musical film. Elegance is lighthearted, joyous, and spontaneous. No crazed declarations of love, no heaviness, just a note of music. So, yes, be surprising if it's life that carries you away but not if it's just an exercise in style.

GOLDEN RULE: A happening not a performance! You improvise and he participates—a duet?—and it becomes a game for two. Not work, which he may watch with dread, wondering whether on earth he should call the cops or the fire department.

Small follies to surprise him with

RENT A CONVERTIBLE CAR for the weekend.

Send him a BUNCH OF FLOWERS.

Book a WEEKEND IN THE COUNTRY, somewhere there is nothing to do but stay in your room.

Come home a bit drunk and open yourself a BOTTLE OF CHAMPAGNE—then, like a Tour de France champion, shake it and give yourself a crazy shower with it!

TURN UP NAKED underneath your trench coat or under your dress.

Decide to BOOK A ROOM at the last minute in a luxury hotel and arrange to meet him there.

Look over your old CDs and play Name That Tune as you DANCE AROUND THE ROOM together.

LEAVE LITTLE MESSAGES for him in a mystery trail, beginning with a card sent to his office.

In general, NURTURE CONTRADICTIONS! You don't usually wear pink? Wear a fuchsia sweater. Continue not cooking but going to the market. Eat organic food and drink vodka. Read classics and celebrity gossip magazines. Love beautiful things without being in any way materialistic. Say, "Tonight I'm not going out"—and then go out. Learn to recite poems by heart and to swear. Doubt nothing and everything. Seem lazy and work a lot. Buy yourself an expensive bag and put it on the ground at the sidewalk café. This is a nonexhaustive list to be completed as you wish . . .

He's as silent as the grave.

When you talk to him, sometimes he seems to come from another planet—it's hard to get a substantive conversation going. And yet, occasionally, there are flashes, outbursts of "I love you," letters, flowers, gifts. You're lost.

Two possibilities: Either this silent man is just a guy who doesn't think about anything and has nothing to say—in which case we recommend you go directly to page 64 for suggestions on how to leave him—or he is not at ease with the female sex, in which case all is still to play for! There are mute men, just as there are those who are terribly clumsy—"I chose this color because it makes you look slimmer"—and it can be tamed.

In a couple, each needs to learn the other's language, what each considers proof of love. Perhaps for him it is just being there, silently sitting next to you on the bed watching a documentary about animals? And perhaps for you it's pretending to be a manta ray exploring the surfaces of his body.

GOLDEN RULE: Don't force anything. If his silence irritates you, don't try to change him abruptly; rather, tell him gently that you need some animation and then go out to join your friends! Hopefully contact with you will change him a little.

He wants a Birkin bag too!

Your guy wants season tickets to the ballet. He also loves beautiful materials and expensive haircuts, and pays close attention to everything you wear. Compared to those men who throw their clothes in a ball at the foot of the bed before putting them back on the next day, this new lover is not the most classically masculine man.

Though customs have evolved and you have the right to change a tire, ride a motorcycle, and dress like a boy all while completely retaining your femininity, a Parisian man is still expected to be a bit hard, dirty, bearded, with dry eyes. How silly! Behave like you're in Paris, where not far away, Louis XIV danced in a golden tutu, the poet Mallarmé wept for his past loves, and Baudelaire was obsessed with his clothes, proclaiming that dandyism was "the last heroic act"!

Let your man be a sensitive human being, curious, gentle, and tender. What's important is not virility but otherness. Yes, you are able to do everything alone, but you need to be two to kiss and to support each other. So, no worries . . . as long as he gives you a pricey Hermès Birkin bag as well!

GOLDEN RULE:
Virility is not found where one thinks—it is not a matter of muscles or of engine size. Virility consists of courage, including the courage to not be scared of being ridiculed. A true man assumes his own tastes, however unusual, and his own fears, however idiotic—yes, an "I'm scared at the top of a ladder" can make you go weak at the knees.

The first vacation

Parisian Tip

RESORT ON THE BEACH

To be sure of a good vacation, book a group trip to a beachside resort! You get the best of both worlds: Privacy is yours when you need it—romantic interludes in your room, spontaneous trips out for just the two of you, and room service at any hour, but also laughter with friends beside the swimming pool, mad chases through the hotel corridors, and big drinks at the lobby bar.

It is not unusual for a couple's first vacation to be imperfect. Totally normal! The first vacation is like the first trip to IKEA: guaranteed arguments. You were waiting for that trip impatiently, you imagined being naked on a deserted southern beach, sun, sea, and kisses. But you are so eager for everything to be perfect that every decision—in the shower or on the bed, beach or pool, mussels or tapas?—becomes an international incident. After three days it all blows up. You scream at each other in the middle of the night, and you end up sleeping under a blanket on the terrace like an idiot before returning to bed when it starts drizzling.

And so? Just as you didn't set off for the beach in Louboutin shoes, don't take crazy demands with you. Your dream is for the two of you to do nothing? Begin by simply doing nothing, and that's it! Stop planning.

GOLDEN RULE: Don't devise perfect vacations all by yourself as if you were the heroine—that's the best way to make your man moan because he will have no other role than to judge! Another vital factor is not to plan a vacation for longer ahead than you have already spent together. You have been together six months? Don't plan for next year.

The Parisienne's holiday bag

FOR THE BEACH:

A GOYARD bag or a pretty recycled tote bag.

A COTTON COVER-UP.

An ERES swimsuit.

A pair of PERSOL glasses.

A WIDE-BRIMMED HAT or a Panama (Maison Michel or, for a more affordable version, Atelier Théodore).

ESTHEDERM sun cream. Take the sun in moderation and occasionally slip a few drops of tanning lotion into your night moisturizer for a slightly tanned skin when you wake up.

FOR THE BEAUTY ROUTINE:

Remove makeup with CRÉALINE H2O BIODERMA micellar water. If necessary, smear yourself with CLARINS Anti-Thirst mask as emergency treatment under the shower with a CAUDALIE Crushed Cabernet exfoliator.

Don't shampoo often; rinse your hair with a detangler and apply CHRISTOPHE ROBIN'S Lavender Oil. For hairstyling, let the wind do its thing as you sit at the wheel of your Citroën Méhari!

FOR THE EVENING:

Your MASCARA (see the Parisienne's makeup bag, page 81).

A little GUERLAIN TERRACOTTA that you apply by drawing a figure-eight; for the lips CHANEL ROUGE COCO lipshine, ELIZABETH ARDEN Eight Hour Cream, or DR. HAUSCHKA Lip Care Stick.

If you want, put on a BULY 1803 nonalcoholic perfume (from a magnficent nineteenth-century dispensary revived by Victoire de Taillac and her husband—alias Mr. Cire Trudon, of the candlemaking company—at 6, rue Bonaparte, 75006 Paris). And put NUXE Multi-Usage Dry Oil (nonshimmer version) all over.

FOR THE SUITCASE:

Pell-mell: a pair of jean shorts, a white and a blue blouse (Charvet or, more affordably, Uniqlos that don't crease or basic classics from Art or Maison Standards), a short dress from ba&sh or the local market, a long skirt to wear with a tank top so that a bit of skin is always on view, a beautiful belt from St. Laurent or Hermès, or a woven one you picked up in another country, Rondini sandals you can find only in St. Tropez or beautiful Michel Vivien beach sandals, and big Aurélie Bidermann bracelets that you wear for the whole vacation.

He thinks I smoke too much.

Parisian Tip

THE GLUTEN-FREE BAKERY

He's a bit too big? Instead of telling him he's getting a belly, you broadcast the fact that your cousin has never been fitter since he stopped eating gluten. No need to tell him he should lose weight.

You can't argue with him: You do smoke too much. Cigarettes are very Parisian chic, and you love to play the worldly woman with a ciggie at night under the old-fashioned lamps of the Bar du Marché. But in the morning you have to admit you are more Billy Idol than Albert Camus.

It's not a question of wrong or right; the question is, at a time of political correctness when everyone plays it holier than thou, you have no desire for your man to give you a sermon. Unless it's in the confessional box? Anyway! Let's not digress. Remind him that he loves you for your free spirit! Show him photos of the great Catherine Deneuve, who always has a cigarette in her lips. If he persists, dare to remind him that for your part you are tolerant and that you don't tell him to go easy on the cheese so he can get that six-pack. And if you become parents, resist the urge to parent each other. You are not there to have a negative image reflected back at you or for each of you to point a finger at the other's excesses.

GOLDEN RULE:
In order to take care of the other or help him kick a bad habit, use the carrot and not the stick. Tell him about his qualities, not his flaws, and about something you both desire rather than reproaching him. You'd appreciate his taking a similar approach where your shortcomings (including smokes!) are concerned.

THE MOTHER CLICHÉ

It's said that men are looking for their mothers and thus like it when women give them a hard time—but it's not true! You never allow yourself to say things you would not allow yourself to say to your friends. For example: "Wow, you're going heavy on the pasta!" or "You shouldn't mop up sauce with your bread." If you want to keep nothing but love in the relationship, begin by at least having the politeness toward the one you love that you have for your friends!

Oh dear, one of his buddies is your ex!

He had insisted, saying it was important to him—so here you are, looking your sexiest, ready to bring on your biggest charm offensive: You are going to meet his friends. And then you get the shock. No sooner have you arrived than your blood freezes. A jerk shouts out, "No need to introduce your girlfriend to me, I've already hooked up with her!" Oh dear . . . you can already imagine them swapping notes on something other than your skills at making crêpes Suzette. Even worse, your whole chaste act is now dead in the water. Rather than the rare gem, you've just become in his mind the friendly little café that everyone loves to frequent . . .

How to get out of it? By owning your life! Yes, before him you knew some of the local guys. So what? Love is always new! Love is always free! Yes, your heart is his (your body too, for that matter!), but your past belongs to nobody but you.

GOLDEN RULE:
Never be ashamed, but don't talk too much, either. Memories perhaps, but elegance above all!

Parisian Tip

THE "I LOVE YOUR EIFFEL TOWER"!

If you sense he's not happy about the idea of your having slept in the arms of one of his friends, hint that you are more satisfied in his and that his iron lady is the most beautiful monument in Paris.

Should we celebrate Valentine's Day?

Some traditions are good. And some clichés are fun. Sure, the sentimental Valentine's Day cards and dates make you feel like you're in a version of *American Pie* wearing a mauve dress and waiting for a quarterback to drive up in a great big car. So what? That's the charm of it!

So yes, of course, you take advantage of the opportunity for you both to take a joint leap into sentimentality, but in your own version, with some distance and some quirkiness. You liven up February 14 by pushing the cliché to the limit. Why not go and dine at a restaurant with white tablecloths and a live band that serenades your table? Or, if you're super flexible, draw a fake tattoo heart with his name on your right buttock. The sillier, the better.

GOLDEN RULE: Valentine's Day is ridiculous? Embrace the American spirit! Get out the Victoria's Secret underwear, have a blow-dry at the hair salon, climb to the top of the Eiffel Tower, and gaze down with the intense expression of a character on *The Young and the Restless*!

LES SECRETS D'UNE PARISIENNE:
Best tourist sites for Valentine's Day

DINNER AT LE GEORGES RESTAURANT: Ignore the pouting hostesses and concentrate on the stunning view from the terrace over the roofs of Beauborg—taking in the Eiffel Tower and the towers of Notre Dame—so as to have the whole of Paris, as well as your man, at your feet! The food is expensive but not bad: don't miss the famous spicy pasta with lobster.
Place Georges Pompidou, 75004 Paris. Tel: 01 44 78 47 99. www.restaurantgeorgesparis.com

DINNER AT CAFÉ MARLY: For the pleasure of being "at the Louvre" while admiring the celebrated glass pyramid of I. M. Pei (don't miss the statues of the Richelieu wing on the way to the toilets!). The menu is unsurprising but very Parisian: tartar, green bean and mushroom salad, avocado/king crab, and macarons.
93, rue de Rivoli, 75001 Paris. Tel: 01 49 26 06 60. www.cafe-marly.com

TAKE A TRIP IN A HORSE-DRAWN CARRIAGE: Opt either for the classic version, which leaves from the Eiffel Tower, or go whole hog with a personalized version that picks you up from your home.

TAKE A TOURIST BOAT TRIP: Preferably when the autumn leaves have fallen (you should also reread Eric Reinhardt's *Cinderella*, which evokes autumn in Paris like nothing else).

WATCH A FILM LUXURY-HOTEL-STYLE: At the Royal Monceau film club, the screening room in the hotel of the same name, huddled up in leather armchairs with a glass of champagne and Pierre Hermé popcorn.
Only Sunday evening. 37, avenue Hoche, 75008 Paris. Tel: 01 42 99 88 48/98 89. www.leroyalmonceau.com

SLEEP AT THE HÔTEL PARTICULIER: A hotel in the heart of Montmartre that belonged to the Hermès family. For a magical memory, dine in the restaurant Très Particulier, nestled between the garden, the sun lounge, and the bar; then enjoy cocktails and then go to one of the five suites. If it's the weekend, you can prolong the magic at brunch the next day (ultimate luxury: the beekeepers' honey is produced on site and the eggs come from the hotel's henhouse!).
23, avenue Junot, Pavillon D, 75018 Paris. Tel: 01 45 44 77 00. www.hotel-particulier-montmartre.com

He wants to live together . . . and so do I!

Parisian Tip

THE WALK TEST

Will he be a good roommate? Finding out is simple: Go walking with him in your future neighborhood one and observe him. What is he interested in, where does he linger, what shops does he notice, what corner café does he love, does he talk to people? To get to know someone, a walk through the neighborhood is better than all the dinners in the world staring into each other's eyes.

You were having a picnic in the sunshine in the park when he suddenly declared he wanted to see you every evening and to wake up with you every morning, that he was out of his mind when he was not in your arms. So, what about living together? And you said yes! But now . . . anxiety rules. What will everyday life be like—the dirty linen, the desire for freedom and for evenings alone with Pascal (the philosopher, not your sports coach) or for painting the town red, but without him? For all these questions, fast-forward to the next section. Love is taking a new turn!

What you must do is enjoy! Being together is everything (and with your combined incomes you can afford more space!). Now you have the possibility of a balcony, a real table where you can eat, a washing machine, dishes, even a walk-in closet. Simple but effective pleasures, like the good old missionary position. So pack your boxes, you're leaving on a journey to a new land.

GOLDEN RULE:
Unless he lives in the apartment of your dreams, you don't go to his and he doesn't come to yours (feelings of suffocation guaranteed). Choose a third place, so that everything that goes into it has been approved by the two of you.

I want to marry him!

Yes, be crazy, get married! But do it in your own way: no bridesmaids, no department store registry, no cheesy band. Instead, the DJ is a friend, everyone is dressed in white, you leave on bicycles, and it's you who laughingly gives him the ring, which you offer on a French fry—and all of it for the joy of being able to say "my husband" and not "the guy I live with" or "the father of my children"! You are crazy and fantastic—marriage will be too.

Parisian Tip

WHERE TO GET ENGAGED IN PARIS

EXOTIC RESTAURANTS:

CAFFÉ STERN, one of the best Italian restaurants in Paris.
47, passage des Panoramas, 75002 Paris. Tel: 01 75 43 63 10.

SOMA, a new, trendy Japanese kitchen.
13, rue de Saintange, 75003 Paris. Tel: 09 81 82 53 51.

THE NEW GENERATION:

LE SERGENT RECRUTEUR, because it's an opportunity to go to the Île St. Louis and because you dine exquisitely well there.
41, rue St-Louis en l'Île, 75004 Paris. Tel: 01 43 54 75 42.

LE CHATEAUBRIAND, for the rocking Basque chef Iñaki Aizpitarte.
129, avenue Parmentier, 75011 Paris. Tel: 01 43 57 45 95.

THE KING OF BARS:

MONSIEUR BLEU, for the Eiffel Tower and one of the most beautiful terraces in Paris.
20, avenue de New York, 75016 Paris. Tel: 01 47 20 90 47.

PARTY LOVERS:

BRASSERIE BARBÈS, for a cocktail, a log fire, and a last dance in the attic.
2, boulevard Barbès, 75018 Paris. Tel: 01 42 64 52 23.

LE DERRIÈRE, for the ping-pong, the terrace, and because it is actress Jessica Alba's home away from home.
69, rue des Gravilliers, 75003 Paris. Tel: 01 44 61 91 95. www.derriere-resto.com

PART 3

Years of happiness!

You've been so immersed in love that you've barely noticed the time flying by! You've entered new territory and you are now in it together for the long haul. You've gone through so much, tamed him, made room for him in your life; and he has done the same for you. You share a home sweet home, perhaps babies and the bliss of life together. Your heart leaps for joy when your man returns after work, the prospect of evenings in your favorite bistros, either just the two of you or with your friends who are now combined, your tender nights that are still sexy—even if you have asked yourself heaps of questions along the way!

How can you keep the element of mystery when you meet each morning around the breakfast table, how to deal with the dirty laundry and the messy bathroom, what do you do when you feel like falling into someone else's arms . . . and, above all, how do you remain two lovers when daily routine insidiously gnaws away at your relationship?

Long-term relationships take work, but you manage it! Your relationship is your own Place des Victoires, the success of a happy life together, made up of magic and also the desire for it to keep on working, again and again, despite the passing of time. "Everyday words seem to turn into love songs"? It's as though Édith Piaf wrote "La Vie en Rose" just for you!

Our four hundredth dinner together

When you were single, you could not have imagined you would dine with the same man every evening without finding it a bit monotonous. You were wrong! Between invitations to friends' dinner parties, take-out at the office at 9 p.m., and the children getting up during the night, you are overjoyed when you can finally be alone together. Dinner for the two of you should be a celebration, like a rerun of your first date but without nervous small-talk or fear of silence—because, contrary to the common preconception, the more you know each other, the more you have to talk about. And how wonderful it is to have your heart start racing when you hear your lover's key in the lock and then to prepare a simple supper together.

In short, with the passage of time you love these moments with him more than ever. As long as you obey certain rules. In the evening you turn off the TV and, ideally, silence your phones. And dine together, just the two of you, at home or squeezed in at the counter of that little bistro down the street. Even if you've already nibbled at the children's dinners, it is out of the question to sprawl on the sofa crying, "You go ahead and eat, I'm not hungry anymore!" You say nice things to each other: "You're so handsome in that shirt!"; you talk about yourself, you talk about him, others, life—because if you've chosen to spend your life with him, it is because you love hearing his opinons and perspectives. These moments of sharing and listening forge a unique bond that makes life as a couple so rich. He is the only one who knows both your boss's flaws and your childhood best friend's greatest qualities, or vice versa!

GOLDEN RULE:

Even if he sometimes bores you with stories about his client meeting, his car being towed, or any other daily hassle, you listen to him. And you encourage him—although not too much if it's really tedious! The important thing is not so much what you say to each other as the act of exchanging—giving each other love and spending time together. And that feeling of melting inside yet again when he orders you a slice of chocolate cake without having to ask, knowing it's your favorite dessert. You know that everything else flows from this give and take. Really *everything* (yes, sex included!).

We didn't go out this week, and nothing's planned for next week. Are we stuck in a rut?

If nothing's planned, take advantage of a bit of respite! It has been ages since you were driven by FOMO (fear of missing out). Leave that to teenagers. Even if you love going out, you don't feel like being queen of the nightclub anymore. On the contrary, relish the fact that for once you have a calm few days alone together! As far as we know, you haven't drunk Tristan and Isolde's love potion—the elixir that makes you enamored of the other for life, no matter what he does. To keep things fresh you need to spend time together and even do nothing together—but do it well.

Going out for the sake of it if nothing really excites you is pointless. There is nothing worse than booking a babysitter for every Thursday evening when all you really want is to share a plate of cheese and crackers and laugh together at a rerun of a classic comedy on TV. Doing nothing is better when it's improvised. That doesn't have to mean early nights: far from it. Have some frenzied games of backgammon, read *The Lover* together (this erotic novel by Marguerite Duras will give you ideas), take a bath. You haven't had the time to do that alone for a very long time.

GOLDEN RULE:
Being really revolutionary is staying under the covers all weekend rather than going to parties night after night during fashion week. And if you are really champing at the bit to get off your sofa, improvise a cocktail party or a dinner on the run with your neighbors—the ones who always open another bottle of Chablis to help the herbal tea go down!

Ten ideas to liven up your evenings

Parisian inspiration for spicing up your nights together!

Five easy ideas for DINNER WITH A TWIST:

Order a PLATTER OF SEAFOOD from L'Huîtrier and tonight you can have Trouville at home!

Serve a PLATTER OF CHEESE, to be washed down with a good red wine you've had for a long time and have not yet dared open.

Go to gastronomic shop Lenôtre and return with a PYRAMID OF SORBETS . . . or a mythical Incredible or Marvelous cake from pâtisserie Aux Merveilleux de Fred. *www.auxmerveilleux.com*

ORDER A HOME CHEF or a meal kit.

TEST OUT A NEW RECIPE by a great chef just for the two of you or as a family and it's *Top Chef* at home!

Five ideas for THEMED EVENINGS:

A FILM EVENING: An Italian comedy with Sophia Loren and Marcello Mastroianni with laughter, stripteases, and Italian pasta.

A CANDLE EVENING: Turn out the lights, switch off phones and computers, light candles, and kiss each other the old-fashioned way!

A THEATER EVENING: Go to the Comédie Française at the spur of the moment.

AN EVENING IN THE BATH: Wait for him in a foamy bath . . .

A "JUST US" EVENING TO REMIND YOU OF THE BEAUTIFUL START OF THE RELATIONSHIP: Invite your beloved to dinner in the wine bar you used to frequent when you first met. Or meet at the five-star Meurice hotel to drink a Bellini or at the Costes hotel for the best mojito in Paris. And check in to spend a wild night?

We've had breakfast together for the past ten years. Where's the mystery?

Mystery is a vital ingredient early in a relationship. When you met, he loved that anecdote about the film awards presentation when you tripped on your evening gown and landed on a famous actor. Now he sighs when you retell it. And when he tells the joke about the pig and the postman, you want to interrupt him and finish it with a botched punchline. The sublime delirium of the early days has long since disappeared. It is less than sublime when the first words uttered in the morning are, "Where did you put my iPad?"

And you know what? It doesn't matter! Mystery is for new relationships; what attracts you now is precisely that marvelous closeness. And so you don't try living in two separate apartments, as actors Pierre Arditi and Évelyne Bouix did for a long time. Distance as the cement that binds a couple together? No, we believe that rarely works. Life as a couple is best lived side by side. Nothing is more seductive than the wink you exchange during a crowded party when you realize you are both laughing at the same thing.

GOLDEN RULE:
Avoid the ugly. While your minds should be up close and personal, remain strangers when it comes to bodily functions: Don't talk about hair waxing or gastric troubles if you can avoid it. And when you get undressed, even if you know each other's bodies by heart, don't show him the pantyhose digging into your waist or your "liberation" from the tight jeans that took twenty minutes to get on that morning.

Seven reasons to look forward to knowing each other by heart

1

Because nothing makes you more in love than feeling understood. Suddenly you don't feel alone anymore.

2

Because the better you know each other, the better you know the little joke that defuses things, the surprise that will make him happy, and the right moment to turn the soft and comfortable bed into a den of pleasure.

3

Because as well as being a lover, he is your best friend, with whom you can do anything and everything together!

4

Because it's lovely to be able to understand each other with just a look or a smile.

5

Because if he holds your hair while you get sick during a hangover, it shows he is in love with you!

6

Because even when you know each other inside out, the smallest new thing can take you by surprise!

7

Because when nothing embarrasses you anymore, you feel confident and liberated.

Feeling playful? Buy yourself a sex toy!

Parisian Tip

THE THEATER EVENING

You don't know how to confess your desire for debauchery to him? Suggest going to the theater in rue de la Gaîté, a neighborhood as hot as Pigalle where there are as many theaters as sex shops. As you come out of a comedy club, it is a good opportunity to go and look, as casually as can be, for an erotic accessory. Two good birds with one stone!

"My meniscus hurts . . ." "Not tonight, I've got an early start tomorrow . . ." "My boss is stressing me out . . ." Sometimes he's the one with the excuses. Even when presented with the sight of you in silk underwear that makes you as sexy as the stunning Isabelle Adjani in *One Deadly Summer,* he remains ice cold. So, you take things into your own hands.

How? To revive your lovemaking, why not a sex toy? A playful way to break the routine and spice up your amorous games.

Finding one is easy: You can slip it into your virtual basket while doing your online shopping! And if you want to feel the latex and see the merchandise for real, take your guy to the local sex store as an amorous exploration, or go alone—but not with your girlfriends. The purchase of a sex toy is not a Tupperware party; it's something deliciously exciting and fun for you and your partner to share.

GOLDEN RULE:
Do not be afraid to shock him with a garter belt, geisha balls, or a nurse's uniform! Your man should never be offended by your attempts to spice up your love life. On the contrary. At worst, you'll both laugh about it—how does this thing go on?—which also brings you closer together!

He hates my collection of flats.

At first he found your shoe collection, with its young-ballet-student look, sweet. But today he can no longer bear your shoes. Tell yourself it's not a metaphor for your relationship. Perhaps deep down he's right and you yourself even agree—they're certainly not sexy. But, in principle, you don't drop something just because your partner doesn't like it. Staying true to your peculiarities is one of the secrets of couples who stay together.

So don't throw out your shoe collection! You play it like Audrey Hepburn in *Funny Face*, shouting "Bonjour Paris," with flats on your feet. Make them sexy by choosing ones that reveal most of your toes, and marry them with a pair of boyfriend jeans or a little dress or a silk camisole that gives a glimpse of bare shoulder and the swell of a breast.

GOLDEN RULE: Loving each other means "loving each other nonetheless," as the French pop singer Pascal Obispo put it. In other words, love each other despite what you think you don't love in your partner. So, cultivate your flaws. In the end, flaws are what make an exciting love story.

Parisian Tip

LA BELLE OTERO

Imitate the Spanish courtesan who reigned over Paris at the time of the Belle Époque. No matter what she wore, she knew how to make the outfit she was wearing devilishly sexy with a diamond between her breasts—breasts so perfect they were said to have inspired the dome of the Carlton hotel in Cannes. Transcend your basic look so that no man at the party will remember anything other than your sensual dancing! Don't judge a woman by her cover.

Should I dress up on weekends?

Parisian Tip

CHRISTMAS WINDOWS

Transform yourself once in a while and make him dream! Emulate that great Parisian tradition in which the big department stores get all dolled up once a year for the Christmas festivities. From time to time, go out dressed to impress! When you appear looking divine from your glamorous hair to your sequined dress, your man will feel like it's Christmas!

After five weekdays of looking your best and putting your mascara on in the rearview mirror without smudging, the impulse to throw on an old, holey sweater on Saturday is very understandable. But even if you are just staying at home with your love, it's out of the question to let yourself go completely. Cheat with a comfortable sweater that leaves one shoulder bare, nipples showing beneath a loose T-shirt, or one of his Egyptian cotton shirts that you wear as a very short dress. Add a bit of under-eye concealer and blush: It only requires five seconds but takes five years off you!

As good Parisiennes, we keep the bittersweet song by Charles Aznavour in mind, "You've Let Yourself Go," which acts as a deterrent for us: "You know, you'd lose a little weight/If you would watch all that you ate?/A little style, a little grace./And try to show a smiling face." To avoid such reproaches, be careful. Avoid spending the weekend in leggings—you get those out for Pilates, period. Take advantage of the weekend to care for your skin, bloom naturally, and display your skill as the queen of understatement. If you're taking a walk in the park, going shopping at the market, or stopping by the bakery, you get ready in a few minutes—but you *do* get ready. A combination that never fails? Shining hair, impeccable nails, and natural-looking foundation.

Coming for a run, darling?

When you met him, he used to sail, steering a boat into the setting sun with the effortless cool of French actor Alain Delon in *Plein Soleil.* Ten years later, he is still as attractive—although less and less like Alain Delon. Eating multiple meals out each week, combined with indulging in cheese platters and his favorite guilty pleasure, chocolate croissants, have taken their toll; and he's complaining about feeling a bit fleshy. Which is why last week he asked for your advice on how to get rid of love handles. Depressing? On the contrary, it's seductive that he wants to take care of himself after so many years together.

There are several options. You can love him as he is, with his (very) little paunch. A man who isn't skin and bones is sexy to touch. And so you leave him be with his cream in his coffee!

Or you can be supportive as he gets back on track. It's true that a few extra pounds a year is not much, but you have been together for ten years—do the math. So you help him. But not any old way. Avoid Swedish fitness classes together where you watch each other failing to perform ten push-ups, or Bikram yoga—sweating en masse is for group sex. But do encourage him. When he goes out jogging, applaud his determination without mentioning his outfit. And when he comes back, all sweaty, jump on him.

He still goes to a nightclub every Thursday.

Let's be frank, you prefer a guy who still wants to go out rather than one who returns home at the same time every evening to put on his slippers. However, his continued insistence on maintaining the sacrosanct Thursday "old buddies" night begins to wear thin. Like the immutable poker evenings. But you won't change him—which is just as well because it's wonderful to be with a man who is young at heart!

How to live with it? First, by not being jealous: Just because he is going to a nightclub doesn't mean he is going fishing for a catch! In any case, real cheaters would look for opportunities even at the supermarket. Secondly, take advantage of his love of nightlife. His evenings on the dance floor have made him into a fabulous DJ? That's also why your friends appreciate your parties and are even impressed that you continue to organize them. And his nights out are opportunities for you to spend time nurturing your friendships, getting together with an old friend over cocktails, or living it up at a fancy nightclub. It's not a competition, but all the same it's important to have your own fun. Finally, if you are in a lazy phase, take advantage of the opportunity to have the house to yourself: Enjoy a warm bath with a good book and that unflattering mud mask—perfect for improving your skin, but not such a good look to sport in front of your man!

GOLDEN RULE:
Just as Paris will always be Paris, he will also always be the same. Don't berate him. And remember that you were drawn to him in the first place because of his youthful energy—which he has not lost.

Parisian Tip

RIGHT BANK, LEFT BANK

In Paris the Right Bank and the Left Bank have distinct reputations. Each is unique, distinguished by its own history and character. Facing each other and also soulmates, Right Bank and Left Bank see each other every day, complementing each other without merging into one. It's the same in love: Each of you has your own style and reputation, and together you make the perfect combination.

Where to take him dancing

If you're ready to put on your dancing shoes, find your own version of these Parisian hotspots.

CAFÉ CARMEN: This historic mansion has been a night spot since 1875, notable for its strange cocktails, its period furniture, its moldings, and its extravagant rococo statues.
34, rue Duperré, 75009 Paris. www.le-carmen.fr

LE BARBÈS, a concept bar where you can tan on the roof terrace, dine in the restaurant, have a drink upstairs in the patio smoking room, and execute a few dance steps under the disco ball!
2, boulevard Barbès, 75018 Paris

LE BADABOUM, a cocktail bar, cozy apartment, and electro scene that makes the whole capital dance!
2 bis, rue des Taillandiers, 75011 Paris. www.badaboum.paris

LE SILENCIO: Join the Parisian arty crowd for a cucumber cocktail at the start of the evening and enjoy a smoking room with trees decorated with driftwood and a dreamlike décor designed by filmmaker David Lynch.
142, rue Montmartre, 75002 Paris. www.silencio-club.com

Taken over by a joyous band of businessmen, CASTEL, where Françoise Sagan and Salvador Dalí used to run into each other, has been brought up to date with its hand-picked members and its erotic décor (go and see the carpet!).
15, rue Princesse, 75006 Paris

Sparkling new, LES BAINS has reopened with a hotel in addition. This space was once a bathhouse used by Proust and later a dance floor for Madonna. You will find a restaurant with an incredible "whale's belly" décor and, in the basement, the club and its famous swimming pool.
7, rue du Bourg l'Abbé, 75004 Paris. www.lesbains-paris.com

LE SYNDICAT, where you can dance while drinking one of the best cocktails in Paris. Very French cocktails from the 1960s, reworked to contemporary tastes, based on chartreuse, blanche d'armagnac, absinthe, and Lillet Blanc. Deliciously retro.
51, rue du Faubourg St. Denis, 75010 Paris. www.syndicatcocktailclub.com

LE MONTANA, where the stars go. Mostly. A very small club at the hotel Montana that lights up the nights on the Left Bank, after a drink at the Flore or on its small terrace.
28, rue Saint Benoît, 75006 Paris. www.hotel-lemontana.com

I don't want to pick up his dirty boxers!

Parisian Tip

THE DRUGSTORE TRICK

Beautifying daily life is also about creating surprises. Think of the Publicis Drugstore on the Champs Élysées, a concept store ahead of its time, open day and night and a real Ali Baba's cave. Here you can buy a last-minute present—a strip of Pierre Hermé macarons, a bottle that brings some fizz into your sitting room, the latest book of photos by street artist JR—while taking advantage of your anonymity (the pharmacist at the Drugstore does not know you). The miraculous potions or lubricating gels, according to the problem of the moment, are all yours.

Intimacy is often filled with micro-responsibilities that cannot be avoided. We are far from the court of Louis XIV, where the royal white shirts were kept in large trunks and changed up to five times a day. Today in order to hide bodily dirt you may find yourself becoming a washerwoman. Does that mean you should have a shared laundry basket? Seeing your lover's dirty boxers abandoned between two crumpled socks is not exactly a turn-on. If possible, we suggest each does his or her own laundry in private. The same for earplugs, anticellulite cream, or his hair-covered razor: They should be kept out of sight. Otherwise you might as well leave the living room with a good book and a roll of toilet paper under your arm. This is not misplaced prudishness—you are the first to enjoy laughing at the dirtiest jokes! It is a question of sparing yourself some of the less-savory habits for the sake of romance.

GOLDEN RULE:
In the event of a faux pas—we leave it up to you to decide what that might be—you never make a drama out of it. You are not rigid and you do not deny the embarrassment. You laugh and move on.

Do you keep count in love?

Once you are sharing a roof, children, and, if you are lucky or have inherited one, a vacation home, how do you organize your coffers? If he is a live-for-the-moment spendthrift and you are a bit of a penny-pincher, or vice versa, finances can quickly become a source of conflict.

While we don't claim to be financial advisers, we believe a joint account is necessary to manage daily finances when you buy your first apartment together or when you have your first child. This also helps to balance out your incomes discreetly if you earn more than he does, or the other way around. The Parisienne, proud of her freedom, makes it a point of honor to share all the family bills. For your personal expenses, having your own bank account is like the basket of dirty laundry: each to his own. Even if your spending is not as extravagant as Marie Antoinette's, your beloved does not need access to the bank statement that reveals that little indulgence at lingerie shop La Perla, the cost of which might seem excessive until he sees you wearing it. The rule applies to everybody: You don't look in his pockets to check out his ATM receipts, the cost of his latest guitar, or his new speakers. A joint account for shared everyday expenses and each your own account for the rest means arguments avoided at the end of the month!

GOLDEN RULE:
Never say how much something you have bought yourself costs—except in cases where you just can't help letting it slip. A surfboard purchased from Australia? The cost of highlights at exclusive hair salon John Nollet? Keep that information to yourself; it's much better that way. Just like the price of the limited-edition sneakers you lovingly place for him at the foot of the bed: He'll proudly enjoy telling his buddies, "My wife bought them for me!"

I was a sex goddess when I was pregnant, now I feel like a nun.

Any time during the first trimester of pregnancy, hormones will turn you into a version of Italian actress Monica Bellucci, breasts on display, libido at its highest, capable of suddenly diving under a porch to satisfy your desires. During the second trimester, although you are getting heavier, it is even better. In the wild heat of the moment, you alternate between tenderness and the most risqué practices, your sensuality at its peak. This is the opportunity to explore the gamut of the *Kama Sutra*. The third trimester is sometimes (not always) less intense. Then, once the baby has arrived, as sleep becomes a rare luxury, the marital bed undergoes a transformation, serving as a place to breastfeed or give a bottle rather than the venue for a torrid encounter. Not to mention, rather than finding a sexy negligee under the covers, you find Sophie the Giraffe and a collection of forgotten pacifiers. The very idea of stretching out in bed for any reason other than to collapse with exhaustion no longer occurs to either of you.

So, how to get back on the ride again? Increase your hugging and kissing, the gateway to awakening a sexuality that has seemingly deserted you. And don't hide behind the baby and fatigue (see the rattle cliché on the following page): Remind yourself that though children will ultimately flee the nest, your relationship will remain. And if all else fails, the prospect of a life without sex should motivate you!

GOLDEN RULE:
Use the technique of "skin to skin,"—placing the newborn against its parents' stomachs—with your beloved. Touching and kissing each other remains the quickest way to recreate intimacy, rediscovering the pleasure of taming each other and making love once more, very gently. It is like the first time, all over again. And it will remove all these little tensions, the ones that are born along with the baby!

The first child: I've been hit by a tsunami!

A strange couple has taken over your bed: Mommy and Daddy. The crazy part? They are you! Nobody is prepared for such a dramatic shift. True, the Parisienne—that strange, multifaceted creature—has a magical quality: She doesn't stop living when she has one child or several. But even the most chic Parisienne will be changed by that gurgling pink or blue bassinet in the corner.

Lift your head up! Look farther than your navel and higher than the cradle, at the horizon of your love. At first, a bit of adjustment is required. So if he hasn't noticed your change of hairstyle or you've failed to notice that he's shaved off his hipster beard, don't worry; your powers of observation will soon return. First of all, make sure your little miracle is in the proper place at night: in his room! So that he at last leaves you to sleep, and climax. If you can't manage to tear yourself away from the baby by yourself, ask your beloved to kidnap you. Occasionally hand over your little darling to whoever is happy to look after him and duck out for a stroll along the water, hand in hand, or even escape for a quick overnight getaway.

GOLDEN RULE: Children are marvelous and transcend the relationship, but make sure they don't engulf it. Each in his or her own place, that is how the family should function. Keep in mind that your man will doubtless admire the mother you have become, but he must also stay in love with the free, lighthearted girl whom he met!

THE RATTLE CLICHÉ

You don't go out anymore? "It's because of my children," you think. False! That's a pretext. If you don't go out anymore, it's because you don't much feel like it anymore, and the baby serves as your cover!

His presents are great . . . once in a while.

He never forgets a birthday, but unfortunately, like the famous novelist (and ex-husband of actress Jean Seberg) Romain Gary, who gave all his mistresses appalling gifts from a craft shop in the rue du Bac where he lived, he rarely hits a bull's-eye. Last Christmas he tried a personalized work of art: an Andy Warhol–type photo of both of you in fluorescent pink (a fiasco). And what to say about that tiny skirt you can't zip up (even if you are flattered that he described you to the sales associate as "very, very slim"—proof that he still fantasizes about you!). Not to mention that gift voucher for an induction cooktop . . . Whatever the present, he never quite gets it right. And it's out of the question to ask him to exchange things: He's a very sensitive guy.

Okay. Instead of giving a forced smile that makes you look like a Chucky doll, you tell him you love him. And you adopt the decade theory: For your thirtieth, fortieth, fiftieth, and so on, you control the gift, not very discreetly, by making a list like a child does for Santa. It's only once in a great while, and so you deserve it: "I'd really like a ring with precious stones, snakeskin shoes, and a silver cuff bracelet." For the other years, you leave him to it and laugh it off; after all, it's great to have a guy who loves giving you pleasure and whose clumsiness ensures you have the best jokes of the evening.

GOLDEN RULE:
Be honest: You also get it wrong sometimes (he seemed surprised when you gave him that mustard-yellow polo shirt!).

Quickies are good, any time of day!

These days, you have washing-machine cycles on your mind, not sexual positions! So instead of making an umpteenth list of household tasks, make a list of your fantasies. That's more playful! Say yes, in principle, to everything related to sex in a relationship. The more you practice, the more you want to. You no longer have the time, as you did at the beginning, to exchange languorous French kisses like in the famous Times Square V-J Day photo *The Kiss* or to sigh with love on the Pont des Arts for hours as you watch the sun set over the Seine? There remains a trusty method, a trump card to produce from your sleeve, ideal for overwhelmed Wonder Women: a quickie!

A little bit of fun in the bathroom, after the shower and before dinner? A quick lay after the family lunch and before you all go out to a children's show? Or in the tool shed at the vacation rental? Don't think twice! You have the rest of your life to become romantic again and rediscover time for foreplay.

GOLDEN RULE:
Every opportunity is a good one! Because the days when you had the whole afternoon to light scented candles, run a warm bath, and rub yourself all over with perfumed oil are gone; and because we never have enough time in the day—if you feel like it, don't deprive yourself: Just go for it. If you really want time, treat yourselves to a night of love at a hotel: (see page 51 for inspiration). It's a good ritual to establish!

Am I dreaming, or has he turned into the nanny?

Once you've had a child, the rules of the game change. Terrace cafés late at night with Vincent, François, Paul, and the others become teatimes in the Jardin des Plantes, baby bottle in one hand and biscuits in the other.

And while you may be on fire to go back to your old habits—a café breakfast with your girlfriends and dinners outside now that you can have a few drinks again without feeling guilty—your lover has turned into Mrs. Doubtfire, baby book in one hand, a diaper in the other, and a supply of pacifiers tied around his neck with some organic string. He no longer wants to put a sneakered toe outside, preoccupied as he is with being Super Dad. It's wonderful to see him so invested, but how to get him out of discussions about the pros and cons of baby Tylenol and when to begin sleep training?

First of all, there's no need. Leave him to it. Then draw up, together, a flexible program. Babysitters and daycare are there to provide help, and you shouldn't have to develop a complex about this. All willing hands are welcome, and godfather or mother-in-law can take the little marvel under their wing while you take your man to a sushi lunch. Or send him to the bar with his friends to watch the ball game—he had forgotten he was dying to do that again!

GOLDEN RULE:
Confronted with a case of a husband-turned-man-nanny, apply a fundamental rule that works for bringing up the children, or for cooking or decorating the apartment: Whoever does it is right. And so, if he wants to dress your little girl in a pair of tights that clash with her dress, it doesn't matter. But that also has to work in the other direction. You are organizing the vacation on the south coast all by yourself? No criticism on his part! And congratulate each other. If you want to let slip a little barb about the color of the shelves he chose for the nursery, you should have been there when he did the choosing! In short, stay joyful and life will be all the more radiant!

PARC

I admit it—I find him sexy on a scooter.

Technically, seeing the man of your life on a scooter (especially one that belongs to your first-grade son and is *way* too small for him) should be a touch ridiculous and not very sexy. However, it's far from a turn-off. Even better, it turns you on. Have you lost your head?

No way! In Paris, if you see a man on a scooter it's because he's just taken his brood to school, to an Italian Renaissance sculpture workshop at the Louvre, or to the mini-farm in Saint Cloud park. Men who take care of their children are sexy! The studies prove that when tasks are shared between men and women, whether in terms of housework or looking after the children, their sex life distinctly improves. Oh, if you had only known that watching him vacuum would one day provoke torrid impulses in you!

GOLDEN RULE: Once and for all, get clichés or antiquated stereotypes out of your head about what a man should and should not do. He can do tap dancing, collect teaspoons, or be a quilting ace and still be sexy. It's all a question of perspective!

The other day I felt like screaming at him!

You feel like a sniper in an ambush. You are on the verge of screaming at him, like Paul and Blandine in Sacha Guitry's film *La Poison*, that couple who have been married for twenty years and can no longer bear each other but do not know how to end the relationship. Though you and your man adore each other, sometimes things skid off the rails. Talking to each other kindly has become an art that is harder to master than embroidering French couture.

So what should you put up with? It depends on the relationship. Some couples will not take offense at a "Get out of here, you useless jerk"—they'll be kissing passionately five minutes later. Others demand a divorce after a simple "Beat it!" In short, it is for each couple to define the mode of operation.

Keep in mind that practicing courtly love, in which medieval lovers read each other poetry rather than flinging poetry books at each other's heads, cannot do any harm. But, above all, set your own limits and respect them. Once they are acknowledged, nobody crosses the line! Finally, think of the false insult that gives relief while making the other smile, along the lines of calling him "little idiot" or saying, "You're a real pain in the ass, but the worst thing is, I still love you."

GOLDEN RULE:
Insults are a no-no: They are sordid and they bring you both down. Nothing personal and nothing cruel, ever. A single exception? In bed! The only place you allow yourself to be aggressive, by turning it into sexual ardor, is under the covers. Another exception, of course, is behind the steering wheel. But, in Paris, that's a given!

He wants the children to learn Chinese!

Trying to agree about how to bring up children can create a divide—or even a gulf as deep as the catacombs of Paris. He wants to create little performing animals, competing to enter prestigious schools like the Lycée Louis le Grand, with a place reserved for them in that mausoleum for the famous, the Panthéon—while you are concerned only with their personal fulfillment and signing them up for circus school and art classes. Or all he thinks about is playing video games with your son while, according to the latest school report, there is an urgent need for some trigonometry practice. In short, you are not in sync. And that is normal. It is difficult to always be on the same wavelength when it comes to child rearing.

GOLDEN RULE:
Together, decide on a family motto. After liberty, equality, and fraternity, reading, counting, and greeting is not a bad start. The rest is up to each individual couple.

But you have no choice: Bringing up your brood is easier when the two of you are working together. It's even a question of keeping your sanity. Between the oldest, who refuses to do his homework, and the youngest, who follows you around reciting her grammar, you need each other and, as in the trenches, you must present a united front! You never contradict each other in front of those crafty little beings, even though it might mean you are at each other's throats once they are tucked in bed. You stand together and that brings you closer together.

LES SECRETS D'UNE PARISIENNE:
Take advantage of the cultural capital that is Paris and throw yourselves into it together. The latest exhibition at Centre Pompidou? Perfect for the start of geometry in third grade with its Calder mobiles. Ditto for the origins of artistic perspective in sixth grade and the marbles at the Rodin Museum. Tell yourself that each of you gives the children different aspects of culture that are complementary rather than opposed. Paris is multifaceted, and so are your kids.

Keeping the children occupied? Follow the guide!

Look to these Parisian activities for inspiration

THE PHOTO WORKSHOPS of the European House of Photography. Exhibition visits with guided tours. Just next to the museum, the Ateliers du 12 offers mini courses with artists for youngsters aged six to fifteen.
57, rue de Fourcy, 75004 Paris.
reservation@mep-fr.org

DEYROLLE: A magnificent shop filled with stuffed animals to discover upstairs—lions, swans, white bears, butterflies of a thousand hues. In the bookshop, pretty coloring books.
46, rue du Bac, 75007 Paris. Tel: 01 42 22 30 07.
www.deyrolle.com

LUMINOR CINEMA, in the Marais, taken over by film director Bertrand Bonello, with an excellent children's program and a Childhood in Cinema festival.
20, rue du Temple, 75003 Paris. Tel: 01 42 78 47 86.
www.luminor-hoteldeville.com

CLUB POP MUSIC LESSONS with the artist Constance Verluca. Here there is no music theory. Instead, the children shake their tambourines or bang their drums to pop-rock songs, all together like a real band.
www.leclubpop.com

Where to take them for lunch, brunch, or tea

LÔ SUSHI RESTAURANT, with its conveyor belts from which little hands can choose the appetizing plates of sushi-makis, avocado or prawn salad passing in front of them, this spot is a guaranteed hit!
8, rue de Berry, 75008 Paris. Tel: 01 45 62 01 00.

LUNCH AT FERDI: Children love it, with its crazy burgers, and collection of little cars and toys to play with (and great cocktails for the parents).
32, rue du Mont Thabor, 75001 Paris. Tel: 06 51 70 29 70.

SCHWARTZ'S DELI: For a change from burgers, beat a path to these bagels like they make them in New York. Children love them too. You just have to choose the area: Trocadero, Ternes, or Saint Paul.
www.schwartzsdeli.fr

BRUNCH AT CAFÉ DES TECHNIQUES at the Arts et Métiers museum, where you can enjoy a fantastic buffet and then visit this unique place, created during the French revolution, and admire Foucault's pendulum, the robot house, and other fascinating exhibits.
292, rue Saint Martin, 75003 Paris. Tel: 01 53 01 82 01.
www.arts-et-metiers.net

Oh dear, the nanny is stunning!

When the nanny showed up for her interview, you almost slammed the door in her face! The young lady—born in the year of the 1998 World Cup—was as beautiful as an angel. You felt like her grandmother. It is impossible to live with this Lolita, constantly reminding you you're not twenty anymore and that you have just started dyeing your gray hair. Not to mention that all your girlfriends would tell you you're a lunatic if you let this pretty wolf into the sheepfold, while reminding you of the most famous celebrity divorces involving nannies.

And yet you went ahead and hired her. Because, like a good Parisienne, you are cunning, magnanimous, and visionary. You realize it will be rather pleasant to show off with this goddess who will elevate the décor of any trip to the sandbox in the park or beside the pool in Ibiza. But, most importantly, the message is clear: Choosing this girl is proof of a wonderful confidence in yourself, your husband, and your relationship. And that you, the fulfilled and radiant young mother, are not threatened by an incredible young woman.

GOLDEN RULE:
Fear gives bad advice. Don't show that you are threatened—and anyway, you're not. The Parisienne adores a challenge. You just add a little emphasis to that toss of the shoulder and your languorous gaze, and you don't hold back with loving words and affectionate gestures. And you handle things so well that it's not your guy the beauty falls in love with, but you!

I want to cheat on him.

Parisian Tip

TOSSED BUT NOT SUNK

Think of the beautiful motto of Paris, "She is tossed by the waves but does not sink," and of its coat of arms, with an ancient sailing vessel on those waves. This is like a couple who, even though they may sometimes be tossed about by a little temptation, do not sink. And that makes us stronger.

As a true Parisienne, you snub men who hit on you. However, seeing your single (or not) friends enjoying multiple conquests or watching lovers smooching on the public benches reminds you that your guy is likely the last man you will sleep with, and that scares you. You think of the intoxicating first emotions: the adrenaline of a rendezvous, butterflies in your stomach, trembling hands, the "For me you are a perpetual revelation," as Napoleon wrote to Polish countess Marie Walewska.

The solution to that itch? Either you stop wondering whether this is your last relationship—who knows what tomorrow will bring, particularly in love?—or you grant yourself a little frisson that does you good without doing any harm. When that handsome bearded guy offers to buy you a drink on the sunny terrace of your favorite bar, share a few glasses of rosé with him, some laughter, and several meaningful brushes against the skin—and then cut it short by disappearing, your cheeks aflame. And savor, as you rush home, the words of Sacha Guitry: "The best moment is when you climb the stairs."

GOLDEN RULE:

Let yourself be seduced and allow yourself a little flutter of the heart. A smile at the guy who lifts his head as you walk past, a wink at the handsome dark-haired man at the coffee machine, a compliment here and there. Being and staying desirable is good for the complexion and the mood.

Damn, I've cheated on him!

This time, you did not turn your back on temptation. You jumped drunkenly into the bed of a beautiful stranger. Now what?

Without playing the moralist—a Parisienne does not do that—we try not to cheat on our partner, if only because it is out of style. Middle-class adultery is so 1970s! You don't play the ménage à trois card, like in Claude Sautet's *César and Rosalie*, in which Romy Schneider introduced her lover and her husband without batting an eye. Today, nobody is forced to stay; and if you cheat too much, you leave.

But what should you do in the case of a misdemeanor? Nothing. Don't even talk about it to your best friends so as not to give the affair any reality. But do ask yourself the right questions.

GOLDEN RULE:
Avoid saying, "I cheated on you," but if the digression is a meaningful one, you admit, "Things aren't good at the moment. We need to work through some things." As people rarely cheat on someone for no reason, it's an opportunity to take stock and identify what is missing in terms of the health of your relationship.

It may be a one-time accident. It's crazy how things can quickly escalate from accepting a last drink to ending up in the attic room of a handsome student . . . You are carried away by passion for an entire night. And then you forget it.

Or it's a revelation that you haven't dared admit to yourself: All is not well with your relationship. In this case, you leave the passing lover and the husband, and you start again from scratch . . . at the beginning of Part 1.

Or, last possibility and the most serious, it is the beginning of a real relationship. In that case, things will be complicated for a bit as you sort out your affairs. But once things are in order, be joyful! And let's meet at the beginning of Part 2!

THE "WE TELL EACH OTHER EVERYTHING" CLICHÉ

It is a bad idea to share every little detail of your lives! Be completely transparent with your financial adviser if that appeals to you. But with your partner? Out of the question. Don't boast about having been hit on—he will notice that by himself. And spare him your qualms—"We don't laugh anymore." Instead, find ways to reintroduce a playfulness and lightness to your relationship.

I think I'm dreaming of a house in the suburbs.

The suburbs? Say yes if they're the tree-lined streets of Brooklyn. If not, no. The Parisienne never goes for half-measures. So when you're sick of being stuck on the embankment in a traffic jam, sick of the Marais (impossible to park there!), sick of the big boulevards with no green spaces and neo-bistros you have to book three months in advance . . . you go, yes. But far away! Us, we're going to Marseille! The true Parisienne sometimes emigrates, all the better to return: After all, Coco Chanel shone in Biarritz, Françoise Sagan played in Normandy, and Colette dreamed in Berry. Our only point of divergence from these illustrious compatriots? We reject places where you can't go swimming in January! So, Marseille, here we come!

And what do you do down there? You don't give up your job. You work remotely and return to the capital from time to time, where you enjoy drinks with girlfriends in your old haunts. The rest of the time, you enjoy the south and the Mediterranean, picnicking in coves like those in the film *Marius and Jeannette*. You read a book on a blanket as the children play in the grass, before the diving lesson for which you've both signed up. Are you still a cosmopolitan woman? Yes, because being a Parisienne is above all a question of your frame of mind. It is style, freedom, and adventure . . . a desire to reinvent oneself.

GOLDEN RULE:
Don't become a local—export Paris instead!

Paris in your bag!

Little ways to infuse your life with Parisian charm

TRUDON candles

CARAVANE pillows

Beauty products from the **SANTA MARIA NOVELLA** line

AESOP RÉSURRECTION AROMATIQUE hand washing gel

A **SUBSCRIPTION TO *LE PARISIEN*** to read on the terrace with a little espresso (in the sun!)

A **KURE BAZAAR** ecological nail polish in case you can't find the right shade at the local manicurist.

A beautiful notebook from **ASTIER DE VILLATTE**, the chic tableware line created by two former students of Paris's Beaux Arts school

A **SISLEY PARIS** product like the flower toning lotion, for several drops of affordable luxury

Sometimes I'm scared we're drifting apart.

Parisian Tip

JULY 14

Every July 14, a parade fills the Champs Élysées in celebration of Bastille Day. Fighter jets spit out blue, white, and red plumes of smoke; École Polytechnique students march in formation; and fireworks light up the city . . . And, every year, we find it moving! It's the same in a relationship: Cherish your anniversaries, the day you met, your first kiss, Valentine's Day, whatever—invent your own list of joyous dates to celebrate!

A relationship that lasts is an adventure with endless twists and turns. The total urbanite with whom you fell in love has become a fan of fly fishing? The former clubber has bought himself an entire cyclist's kit (when men's cycling tights just don't do it for you)?

Don't panic; this distancing also has a good side. His overwhelming passion for the bicycle will leave you exquisitely free in the afternoons. How good to be able to reread Patrick Modiano without having to listen to him gripe about how *In the Café of Lost Youth* is a real pain in the ass. Let him enjoy his cycling outings and, mind and calves well aired, he will come back more cheerful and talkative than the wonderful Nobel laureate Modiano.

However, beware of any extreme separation (for example, sound the alarms if one day he is carried away by his bike to a neighboring town where he sets up a panini restaurant). To reestablish your connection, find a shared project. It is for you to decide what it is—planning that round-the-world trip you have always dreamed about, investing together in a little bistro, volunteering with that humanitarian organization so dear to your hearts, organizing a big fancy fund raiser. But pump the brakes if you're considering another child! No, don't be foolish! A child is never a way to get closer.

GOLDEN RULE:
Do not fall victim to nostalgia. The worst thing is to judge what is happening now by the lights of what happened at the beginning of your relationship. A relationship evolves, and so do you. And having your own hobbies and interests will only make you better partners. So take new phases in stride and face each turn in the road as a new and fascinating challenge!

Give yourself some luxury bubbles.

How to unwind like a Parisienne

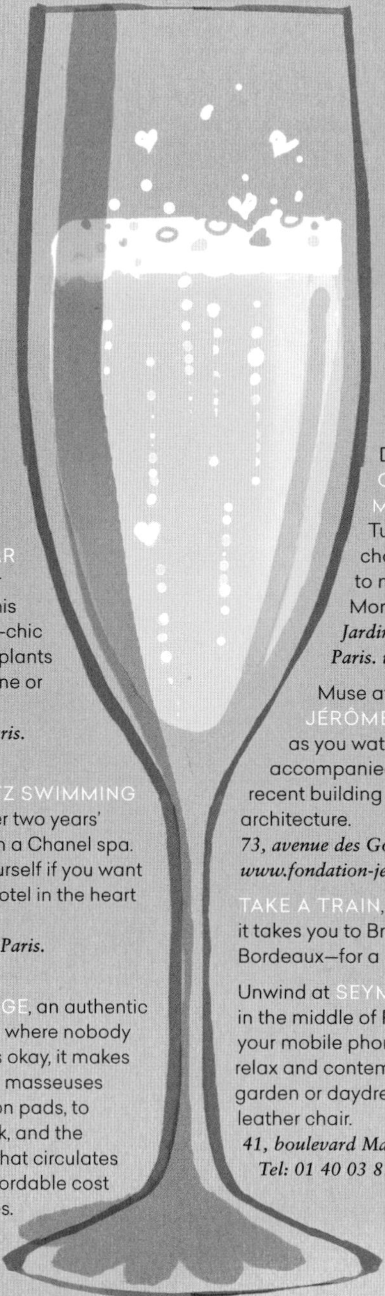

Pamper yourself at the SIX SENSES spa. Nestled between the Place Vendôme and the Tuileries gardens, this spa is a haven of softness. Head or back massages provide total relaxation. In addition, you can drink ginger tea with sugar or honey from the hive installed on the terrace, while gazing at a wall on which a video of the Paris skyline and the Tuileries is projected.
3, rue de Castiglione, 75001 Paris. www.thewestinparis.com/en/six-senses-spa

Try out Leonor Greyl's BAR À BEAUX CHEVEUX for a dazzling treatment in this temple of luxury. The eco-chic products are made from plants and do not contain silicone or parabens.
15, rue Tranchet, 75008 Paris. www.leonorgreyl.com

Bathe in luxury at the RITZ SWIMMING POOL, set to reopen after two years' work in a new setting with a Chanel spa. A beautiful present to yourself if you want to take a dip in a luxury hotel in the heart of Paris.
15, Place Vendôme, 75001 Paris. www.ritzparis.com

Relax at LANQI MASSAGE, an authentic traditional Chinese salon where nobody speaks French—but that's okay, it makes it all the more exotic! The masseuses artfully manipulate suction pads, to relieve tension in the back, and the gua-sha, a jade spatula that circulates energies. All for a very affordable cost at four different addresses.
www.lanqi-spa.com

Laze about at CHANTELIVRE, ideal for emptying your mind. In this wood-lined bookshop long devoted to children's books, you can return to childhood with a classic, a love story, or a beautiful comic strip. A very lively place thanks to its vivacious staff. A must!
13, rue de Sèvres, 75006 Paris. www.chantelivre.com

Dream at the ORANGERIE MUSEUM in the Tuileries after a hot chocolate at Angelina's, to marvel yet again at Monet's water lilies.
Jardin des Tuileries, 75001 Paris. www.musee-orangerie.fr

Muse at the FONDATION JÉRÔME SEYDOUX-PATHÉ as you watch a silent film accompanied by piano in this recent building with majestic architecture.
73, avenue des Gobelins, 75013 Paris. www.fondation-jeromeseydoux-pathe.com

TAKE A TRAIN, any train—whether it takes you to Brussels, London, or Bordeaux—for a day with a difference.

Unwind at SEYMOUR, bubble of calm in the middle of Paris, where you leave your mobile phone at the entrance to relax and contemplate in the winter garden or daydream huddled in a leather chair.
41, boulevard Magenta, 75010 Paris. Tel: 01 40 03 81 68.

It's awful. I want him to do what I say!

"Can't you wear something other than that old gray hoodie?" you reproach him—and yet he still puts it on every day. "What time are you coming back?" you interrogate him—and he looks at you as if you are his mother. To make him do your bidding without turning yourself into a harpy—because, without going as far as merging your email calendars, you need a bit of organization—what do you do?

It's not in your nature to play the policeman. At first, take care of the schedule yourself. And then, have faith in him: He's not an idiot and he knows you're questioning him not to constantly breathe down his neck but so that family life runs more smoothly. He will end up doing as you ask—but in his own way, showing you that he is also capable of making the decisions.

GOLDEN RULE:
The less you nag him, the more he will feel like they're his own decisions, and the more he will help you! So stand back a bit and busy yourself with other tasks. You have far better things to do together than bicker over scheduling! Fewer fights means more time to love each other!

THE PANTS CLICHÉ

You've heard it a million times: In a couple, there's always one partner who wears the pants. One commands and the other obeys? Not true! Most of the time, for a relationship to work, each of the partners must have the impression he or she is in control. That is the secret of equality.

He wants me to get my breasts done.

We have a French saying that goes, "A woman marries hoping her man will change, and he doesn't change. A man marries hoping that his woman won't change—and she changes!" Your man suddenly has the fantasy of you becoming a beautiful Italian: Sophia Loren, Monica Bellucci, or Gina Lollobrigida, overflowing your white bustier. If it's something you really want to consider for yourself, make an appointment with the plastic surgeon to talk about the possibility of increasing your bust size. Perhaps, deep down, you have always dreamed of yourself stretched out on that Corsican beach, your new breasts as curvaceous as the dome of the Invalides. Fortunately, this moment of madness soon passes because you realize you're gorgeous just the way you are. Small breasts are sexy—plus you can go braless under your Yves Saint Laurent suit. So in the end of course you say no—we like ourselves as we are, thank you.

GOLDEN RULE:
Don't take what he says personally. Instead, listen to what he really wants. Rather than changing your body, explore zones where you have never yet ventured!

But you pay attention to the suggestion behind the request: "I still love you, I still desire you, but I want change." You hear his desire for new fantasies surge up. So you book a room at a luxury hotel, surprise him with your sex shop purchases, and spend the night acting out all your wild fantasies. He's going to get some of that promised change!

He looks more and more like George Clooney.

When a third girlfriend whispers to you, "Your guy is aging well," you start paying attention. And you become a little wary. It's true that he's even more gorgeous with his beard and his graying temples. And you? You feel like that while time has stopped for him, it's racing forward for you! While he is getting more like George Clooney, you are turning into Simone Signoret in her *Madame Rosa* period!

You must shift your perspective! Getting old is, above all, a state of mind. Avoid going to extreme lengths to keep your youth—like Diane de Poitiers who, to attract Henri II (twenty years younger than she!), drank pure gold as it was supposed to be an elixir of youth. She was poisoned, and died. Model yourself instead on Romy Schneider, so much more seductive than the very young Jane Birkin in *The Swimming Pool*.

The Parisienne is like good wine: She improves with age. The less you use anti-aging artifices, the more electrifying you are! What counts is posture, the assurance you acquire, and that *je ne sais quoi* that attracts people's gaze . . and it doesn't hurt that you are on George Clooney's arm!

GOLDEN RULE:
You're not jealous of your man's looks! You're certainly happy that he is aging well, but you don't compare yourself to him. The only attitude that works is to make yourself beautiful for yourself. When you feel attractive and confident, others will find it attractive too.

How to look good at forty

At forty years old, you know what suits you and how to enhance your attractiveness; you have edited your wardrobe so only the most flattering items remain. Here are some staple pieces to keep in your closet:

A very soft navy blue V-neck sweater to wear with your favorite jeans

Your grandfather's timeless trench coat

The little black dress that goes with everything

A beautiful dinner jacket

Ultrasexy heels

A man's watch

Faded denim jeans

A leather jacket

A white blouse with pinstripes, worn with jeans

A white T-shirt (ideally by Isabel Marant or Majestic Filatures)

A beautiful striped sweater

A pair of Oxford shoes

Black ankle boots

I'm fed up tonight. Am I fed up with the relationship?

Parisian Tip

THE PARVIS OF NOTRE DAME

In the middle of this huge esplanade bordered by the Seine and the Hôtel Dieu hospital, in the shadow of the cathedral towers, is a medallion engraved with a wind rose, a predecessor of the compass. It is the center point from which all distances to Paris from other places are measured—the nerve center of Paris. From here one can decide to leave for Calais, Menton, or Hendaye. If you feel your relationship has lost its way, rediscover your center point and recenter yourselves where you began, on your founding story. What is it about him that thrills you? Why did you choose him?

It's true, sometimes he tires you for no reason. Bores and stifles you. You find his stories about work tedious, and when he slips his hand onto your lower back, his touch irritates you. And yet normally you are the first to defend the delights of life together, which you liken to the pleasure of eating your favorite treats again and again: a pile of macarons, a crêpe Suzette, some truffade . . . Rather than being a pain, it is even, most of the time, very good. But tonight you're completely fed up with him!

The temptation is to change the restaurant or find another chef to cook for you. But it's a bad idea. You just need a little detox! Organize a trip with an old girlfriend, go and drink a spritzer with your ex-turned-confidant, stroll along the river with your face in the wind. Explore places far from your usual haunts . . . and from him. After this mini break you'll find you miss him again. And your appetite for his wandering hand and the way he looks at you with love will return.

GOLDEN RULE:
When you're fed up, don't force yourself to play nice. Take a break, have fun, and enjoy a change of scenery.

We're so busy, we don't even have time to argue!

The couple that lasts may occasionally want to scratch each other's eyes out . . . But real, passionate quarrels like young lovers? Impossible to squeeze those in between taking the children out to a show, a family brunch, and a birthday dinner for ten! Arguments are a luxury for a young couple with time. Or for stars: Only Godard, passionately in love with Anna Karina, could cut up his own clothes after a fight with her—so as to let off steam without hurting her!

So when do you lay into each other? Make an appointment for lunch. The famous "We have to talk." Find some neutral territory—a little table tucked in the corner of a coffee shop or a booth at the bistro down the street—to work through your grievances. Knowing how to quarrel properly is vital; it lays the foundation for true dialogue. Getting things off your chest rather than harboring frustrations lowers the pressure. And you can have a drink too! After ten minutes spent on the tricky subject of dispute, you will move on to something more pleasant. Because deep down you still have lots of things to say to each other and you have just created the conditions to reconnect. What you were longing for was not an argument but a tête-à-tête, a moment snatched from your busy schedules that is worth any amount of soul-searching.

GOLDEN RULE: Never go to bed angry with each other. And pick your battles. It's okay to argue all night over education reform or your favorite reality TV contestants. Parisians find subjects for debate everywhere. But it's out of the question to scream at each other over an expired passport or who is going to cook the children's pasta shells.

THE PASSION CLICHÉ!

Does passion mean heated arguments? Yes, sometimes, to get over crises—like the time he left your laptop in the train, or when he decided on a whim to leave for a "climbing Mont Blanc weekend" with four buddies, only informing you at the summit, because it was something he couldn't miss. But don't forget that true love is a peaceful daily life!

Proust
UN AMOUR DE SWANN
BAIES

Who should take the first step to make up?

It's been three hours or three days since, all fired up, you've told each other the bitter truth; and since then nobody has said a word. Now you sit on separate chairs, arms crossed and jaws clenched. However, "The pleasure of fighting is in the making up," as Perdican declares to his fiancée Camille in Musset's *No Trifling with Love*.

One of the great joys of the lasting relationship is that resolving arguments is a thousand times easier than it was in the early days of your courtship. You know him so well that you know which buttons to press and how to win back his heart after a fight. Be proud of taking the first step to reconciliation. It's really attractive to be able to park your pride. And it gives you an immense advantage over the resentful sulker! Everybody has their own particular tactics: a sideways glance to make the other smile, a hot text message when he's in the same room to defuse things, or, even better, continuing in silence but using your body to express yourself. You don't say anything but you do everything to him.

GOLDEN RULE:
Keep in mind that in each argument lies the beginning of resolution. Having nothing more to reproach him with means having nothing more to hope or to love. And if things get really stuck? Bring out the humor card. Better, imitation. Do as he does, but comically. Your retake of his surly demeanor on the sofa (inevitably unsuccessful, as you're not comedian Florence Foresti), will slide open his little inner bolt. Bravo!

How can I keep desiring him, after all these nights?

How to keep passion alive: That's the big question, the one that makes young lovers tremble in their boots . . . But not you! You know you just have to watch a steamy film or reread *Dangerous Liaisons* to set your imagination on fire. Your feelings liberated, and your desire awakened, you can now throw yourself on the beast.

So, to begin with, take your time. True, your diaries are a bit busier than those of the sardonic Merteuil and the cynical Valmont, who had nothing else to do than find prey for their lust. Now, you sometimes have to make an extra effort after a day at work, the children's homework, and your boxing class to think about frolicking under the covers. But everything is grist for the mill: a dawn alarm to take advantage of morning energy, an elevator that you stop between two floors . . . Every opportunity to feed the fire is a good one.

GOLDEN RULE:
No more than two weeks without sex! Remember the line of Nicolas Boileau: "Put your work twenty times upon the anvil," which here takes on greater meaning. Practice, again and again!

Then, maybe, spice things up by buying books to try new techniques and feed your own imagination to warm yourself up if necessary! In Paris, it's easy: You need only go see the Watteau nudes in the Louvre to feel excited. And the spark has returned: You just have to see him sitting opposite you at the table to feel like cuddling up against him or even dropping your napkin . . .

Ten things to invite into your bed

We all have lots of imagination, but to spark your creativity, here are some ideas!

A can of WHIPPED CREAM

A tie to COVER HIS EYES

A NEIGHBOR who can see you from afar (but only if you are on vacation, not the neighbor you bump into as you are leaving for work every morning!)

A MALE STRANGER whom you found very attractive and who leaves in the early hours

A FEMALE STRANGER whom you found very attractive and who leaves even sooner

The *KAMA SUTRA*—to look at and to try

A CAMERA or simply your phone

STORY OF O or any erotic book that gets you going

A COSTUME with handcuffs, a maid's outfit, or Wonder Woman gear

MINI SPEAKERS on which, like a couple of teenagers, you play love songs on a loop

I feel like I'm turning into my mother.

Every weekend, it's the same old routine. You nag him to find a babysitter (oh, that crazy desire to meet up with your group of friends as soon as Friday arrives); order him to get a haircut (you can't take any more of that teenybopper hairstyle); send him to the grocery store, but not any old one (the one that carries the organic Breton tomatoes) while he huddles up in front of the television waiting for the tornado to pass. You promised each other the best, but you feel like you've become the worst: his mother (or even your own when you were sixteen). Let's be clear: This is an emergency because if you are his mother during the day, he will soon have a problem at night.

To avoid getting to that point, you have three options. First, ask yourself what is really urgent (will you think about organic tomatoes on your deathbed?). Let go of a few things and suggest he give you a hand with the essential ones (the babysitter!). Second, hand the reins over to him. He is an awful cook but he loves going on a shopping spree at the farmer's market? This time, he can organize the dinner; leave him to it, rather than commenting. The third, and most essential, point: Change your tone. You can say and get everything you want, provided you sprinkle your commands with liberal helpings of "Sweetheart, darling, it would be great if . . ." And, presto, disappeared in a puff of smoke are your mother, mother-in-law, and other mother superiors!

GOLDEN RULE: Lowering the pressure means catching him off guard. He is expecting to have to tame a tigress? Be as gentle as a kitten, affectionate and cheerful, and organize the weekend tasks with a light touch. He will be quick to put his shoulder to the wheel and will tell you to go and pamper yourself at your favorite spa (see page 163).

THE MAMA CLICHÉ

Men want to be looked after? It depends how! Rather than ordering him to put a sweater on—he knows how to read a thermometer—be attentive when he is stuck in bed with a bad cold: a warm bath and a grog worthy of the head barman at the Hemingway, the legendary bar at the Ritz. A mama, no; a geisha, yes! That's much more fun.

Parisienne strategies for lowering the pressure

For a change of scene:

L'AUBERGE DU BONHEUR in the Bois de Boulogne for its name, and for melon beneath the lime trees on the gravel path.

A PICNIC in the Luxembourg Garden. Nibble cherry tomatoes on the wrought-iron chairs beside the magnificent fountain of the Medicis.

Lunch in AUVERS-SUR-OISE, the home of the Impressionists. Full of little restaurants where you can have your fill of pancakes!

The restaurant L'ÎLE on L'ÎLE SAINT GERMAIN for lunch in an interior that is a mixture of Napoleon III and modern décors and in the middle of the countryside where children can run around or have pony rides while parents relax in the sun.
170, quai de Stalingrad, 92130 Issy-les-Moulineaux

THE RESTAURANT LES MAGNOLIAS in the floral park, for this magnificent spectacle of an infinite variety of flowers, its vegetable garden, and its scented garden.
Floral park, route de la Pyramide, 75012 Paris

For geeks:

Fancy some Tropézienne pie, a platter of eclairs, or Lebanese street food? Thanks to the food delivery apps, you can choose your lunch from lots of different addresses and get it delivered while slipping onto the list your favorite piece of terracotta or toys for the children!

Along similar lines, the Deliveroo app is a delivery service uniquely for Paris.

He dreams of becoming a DJ.

He's dreaming of becoming a professional DJ or getting a Michelin star? Super, encourage him! He was right there behind you when you decided to become the new Beyoncé (even if it was only for last New Year's Eve party). And he was supportive when you wanted to return to studying by taking an art correspondence course. So, rather than criticizing, you enthuse!

Even better, you become his muse. Follow the inspiration of Sofia Coppola and her partner Thomas Mars, the leader of the group Phoenix. In a shared collaboration, she directs and he composes the music for her films. So if your man wants to fulfill his childhood dream after working as a lawyer for twenty years, what's the problem? If he dreams of becoming a chef at the historic restaurant Tour d'Argent, his hands bathed in the secret sauce for pressed duck—perfect, he'll also whip up lovely little dishes for you inspired by your tastes. He has a DJ slumbering inside him? Maybe he will make you queen of the nightclubs. While waiting for that blessed day, he can perform on the turntables at your friends' parties. You, not a groupie by nature, can become his agent and propose his musical arrangements to your producer friend. Even if he only sells three records, you will have fought together against the tedium that can set in after two decades. Encourage any change in direction—as long as it isn't conforming to the straight and narrow!

GOLDEN RULE: Never shoot down his ambitions. What is more, you find his creativity amazing. Always be up for it, and he will be more fulfilled than ever. On the other hand, if he wants to move to Hollywood to become Leonardo DiCaprio, discuss it first . . . Imaginative is okay, completely deluded is not!

Is it strange I'm so happy all the time?

Parisians can be appalling grouches. It is their great flaw, a snobbish pessimism that verges on the unbearable. And so if you're a good Parisienne you almost feel bad about your happy love. Forget that attitude! Joy should be assumed with pride! Don't be ashamed of happiness. Think of Esméralda, Victor Hugo's beautiful gypsy who dances on the parvis of Notre Dame. Or of Édith Piaf, who murmured to her handsome lover Marcel Cerdan in the song "La Vie en Rose," "Happy, happy to die of love." Happy! It is all the more use to make smiling, enthusiasm, and gaiety your religion when you live with someone. Because in a couple everything gets more intense, including dark moods.

If you feel ridiculous with your excessive excitement for the tiny garden he created on your balcony or that old copy of *Les Misérables* he unearthed for you at a secondhand bookstore—so much the better! Cherish that giddy feeling. Having fun is the essence of the essence. A joke, a shared smile, a burst of laughter and—presto, gone are the little tensions that were appearing on the horizon. Forget Paris and its cynicism; instead, choose France and its beautiful joie de vivre that enables you, when you come home tired, to see the glass half full—of wine—and to smile. Idiotic? No, it's cause for celebration.

GOLDEN RULE:
One swallow doesn't make a summer. Take inspiration from the mantra "Fake it until you make it." And from Salma Hayek, honorary Parisian, who has the wonderful habit of wishing herself a great day every morning and of thanking herself in the evening! If you believe in happiness enough, it will eventually move in with you.

Using strategy is fine at the beginning . . . but afterward?

Putting on an act to get what you want, not calling so he will be more eager . . . Strategy, you think, is something for a young schemer, and you have no more need of it. Naïve! So have these chapters washed over you like the water of the Seine? Reread page 52: "Strategy? Yes—but at the strategic moment!" That's a golden rule to tape onto your tube of lipstick.

Even if you are proud of your wonderful shared experiences, made up of children, friends, lovers' weekends, or long-distance trips, and of cloakrooms (sorry, we digress), don't rest on your laurels. Find ways to keep him on his toes! For example: Next time you're on business, go out dancing with your coworkers one night. However, you reassure your beloved that (almost) like Cinderella, you came back around 1 a.m. Giving a song and dance about the sexy and fashionable people you were out with will not lead anywhere good. On the other hand, if it's he who's gone skiing with ten party-loving buddies, it's no good whining about being alone with your depressed cousin drinking wine on the couch—instead go out and create your own fun! In short, sometimes putting on a pretense of perfect happiness will translate into real happiness.

GOLDEN RULE:
In a lasting relationship, strategy is not so much about making him come running—you've gone beyond that!—as it is continuing to help him dream. So embellish the little things and magnify the big ones; it's a win-win situation, not least in terms of the health of your relationship. But when necessary you bring out the old recipes. He's not looking at you the way he used to? Let yourself innocently flirt with someone else.

He's suddenly a pro at wild new sex positions. Is he cheating on me?

The two of you are having a passionate evening, foreplay in full swing, when suddenly he asks you to turn over and try a new position: his foot on your hip and your leg around his neck in the "panda position." It's a bolt from the blue despite your many rolls in the hay! What's gotten into him? Unless he's spent the afternoon at an X-rated film or the evening on the Internet, something is up. A mistress?

Don't panic. Either you discover a lewd message on his phone that confirms your doubts—in which case you have a theatrical showdown with him, in a big scene reserved only for critical situations—or he just wants to have fun, to change your routine a little. Okay, he might have done research in a way you'd rather not know about—but that does not mean he deserves to be dragged to the Place de Grève, where public executions used to be held!

GOLDEN RULE:

No untimely jealousy; we know there is more pride than love in jealousy. Don't convince yourself he must have done this with someone else but rather that he wants to surprise you; the more you know someone, the more confidence you have in allowing yourself to be outrageously daring. Accept that invitation to a trip full of debauchery and delight!

Just the two of us?

What if you don't have children? Many great love stories are lived without children. If you think about it, with two of you there are already three involved! The relationship is a third person that you tenderly cherish: There is you, him, and "us." Others form a group with their kids or their work. You have chosen to stay just the two of you, and so much the better! You give your all to it: He is your star, you are his angel, and all the lights of the Eiffel Tower can barely compare to the loving glow you radiate. Love is so complicated and so infinite that you will never get bored.

GOLDEN RULE:
A relationship relies not on children but on what the two of you build together—and you couldn't give a damn about doing what everybody else does. Your love is something that concerns the two of you, a story you invent together. Trust in your creativity!

Famous couples who march to the beat of their own drum

All lovers have their own story, and all lovers invent a world for themselves without caring what others think. These famous couples will inspire you to live your love as you see fit!

BALZAC AND HIS POLISH COUNTESS EWELINA HAŃSKA: This couple went for years without seeing each other and only corresponding—more than 400 love letters in eighteen years, sixteen of which were spent waiting! In the end they married, six months before the death of the genius who wrote *La Comédie Humaine*.

PHILIPPE SOLLERS AND JULIA KRISTEVA: No children, and a love as free as a bird. Fiercely independent, the famous writer and the psychoanalyst see their love as a conversation, a work of art sculpted by time. Faithfulness? They see it as a way in which the unshakable separateness of the other can be harmonized. And they have been married a half century!

BERNARD-HENRI LÉVY AND ARIELLE DOMBASLE: Stunningly good-looking, almost too photogenic, it is as though this couple has decided to have a relationship that is out of time and to live on love, thoughts, songs, and fresh water alone (and in her case, tea and almonds). An ethereal, surprising, free, and crazy love!

VALÉRIA BRUNI TEDESCHI AND LOUIS GARREL: She has a mellifluous voice with a crack in it that is utterly bewitching; his handsome face could stop traffic. And he is almost twenty years younger than she. The director and the actor adopted a little girl and had several happy years together in utmost indifference to what anyone thought!

SERGE GAINSBOURG AND BRIGITTE BARDOT: He sang about their love magnificently in "Initials BB," and she sang with him in the original version of the steamy "Je t'aime moi non plus." This love story between a poet and the most beautiful woman in the world defined an era (though their love affair lasted only three months).

VERLAINE AND RIMBAUD: Poor Verlaine was as ugly as he was married when he fell madly in love with the sublime Arthur Rimbaud, age seventeen, a wild child and miraculously gifted poet. For two years, he and Paul wrote some of the most beautiful lines of French poetry. Until Verlaine, wracked one day with deadly jealousy, ended up shooting a revolver at his Rimbaud in the middle of Brussels. He went to prison and Rimbaud soon escaped to begin wandering the world, his literary career over. "Oh sad, sad was my soul . . ." Yes, but thank you for the poetry!

BRIGITTE AND EMMANUEL MACRON: She was his high-school teacher when they met (and twenty-four years older). Their passion for one another was a scandal, but they braved it together, and eventually came through the other side. With a love stronger than ridicule or conservatism, and still crazy in love twenty-five years later, they became France's first couple when Emmanuel Macron was elected president in 2017.

All our friends are getting divorced. What about us?

"We only love well once," said Mercédès to the Count of Monte Cristo after he spent many nights dreaming about her from prison. And yet in real life, after forty your friends start dropping like flies. All your friends now seem to be saying they can love well a second time or even more! They are all splitting up, as fast as the autumn leaves falling onto the pathways of the Père Lachaise cemetery. The statistics are disheartening: In Paris, over half of married couples end up divorcing. What if you, too, are seized by the call of the wild, the desire for a new life with another lover? Like Johnny Depp and Vanessa Paradis, whose paths have strayed too far apart after twenty years together? Even the most seemingly unsinkable relationship can capsize.

Beware: Divorce can be contagious, and not always for good reason! People who are unhappy, who are going through a storm, always want to pull you onto their raft so they don't drown alone. Once her head is out of the water, the good friend who has gone back to the single life will try to get you to join her to persuade herself she made the right decision! So keep swimming. Protect your own bubble—you alone know what keeps it light and meaningful.

GOLDEN RULE: Regularly examine your relationship and make your choice, freely. Are you staying together out of habit? When he says to you, like Balzac to his Polish countess, "For me you exude the most intoxicating perfume a woman could have" (okay, not quite in those words, of course), do you still go weak in the knees? If yes, the adventure continues full steam ahead, because that's what you've decided!

Test:
Do you still love him?

You are still madly in love if . . .

You wait impatiently for the sound of his keys in the lock.

You manage not to make mincemeat of him when he does annoying things like leaving the toilet seat up, leaving his beard trimmer in the sink, or brushing his teeth with a worn-out toothbrush without seeming to think anything is amiss.

He sends you a text message saying "I'm on my way," and, while you know that means, "I've got two things to finish up," you don't even get annoyed.

You are turned on by his scent when he kisses you in the evening.

You feel like crying when you argue.

You love the fact that the children look like him.

You are dying for just the two of you to go away.

Your heart skips a beat and your stomach tightens when you see a message from him displayed on your phone.

You laugh together, even in the morning, even when you're in a hurry, and even when it's raining.

You adore that he looks out for you with small gestures such as making you a coffee the way you like it.

You still want to send him thirty texts a day.

You take note of that film coming out, that well-reviewed play, or that new restaurant opening, saying to yourself that it's him you'd like to go with.

He's cheating on me. Is it over?

His smartphone beeped while he was in the shower. Under the contact name "Pierre the Plumber" you see the text: "Thank you darling for that fantastic time. I love you. Will ring tomorrow." Your legs giving way and your breathing shallow, you try to take in the news: He loves someone else. How to react? Should you play the ostrich and put your head in the sand? Bad idea. Such notions are based on false wisdom (it's a passing phase, these things happen . . .) and the suffering is mute but nonetheless present. You will spy on him, doubt him, and go crazy—and forget about love!

Confront him? Ask why or how, how many times? It is human to want to know, but in the short term you will have only answers that answer nothing.

Leave? That is the most fatal outcome. If you decide to take back your liberty because he has behaved like a sordid libertine, there is no going back.

Throw him out? That's what we recommend. It allows you to let off steam. And it preserves your pride and gives him the opportunity to fight to return. Beyond your principles and your wounds, you will only know if you want to forgive him the moment you see him on the doorstep, one hand holding a bouquet of flowers and the other on his heart. Peonies, your favorites . . . Is the door opening?

GOLDEN RULE: Reinvent your relationship. Obviously, being cheated on is a betrayal and reestablishing peace is a long road. But the perfect couple does not exist. Nobody can give you advice on the subject; and it might be an opportunity to think outside the box, to create your own pact, and to build a new love story—stronger and even more beautiful.

Parisian Tip

THINK OF BARON HAUSSMANN!

Paris would have remained a small medieval cathedral town with muddy alleyways without the intervention of the Prefect and city planner Haussmann, who decided to give Parisians "water, air, and shade" and magnificent views like the avenue de l'Opéra. Sometimes you have to agree to knock everything down to allow something better to be built. It's the same thing in a relationship. You continue moving forward, you destroy, and you rebuild! The key is knowing how to reinvent yourself.

We've been together twenty years, and I'm crazier about him every day. Am I soft in the head?

"Love passes like a storm," wrote Maupassant. But for you it's been pouring for a very long time, because you still love him as much as you did in the beginning, this tall guy that you ran into one day outside your favorite restaurant. Perhaps even more. You have faced all sorts of difficulties together and you have become something of a model couple to your friends, who are in awe of how long you have stayed together and how light your inspirational relationship still is, facing life together hand in hand. Love is an art that you have mastered—fantastic, celebrate!

But you are not soft in the head. Loving him as much as yesterday but not as much as tomorrow doesn't make you into a naïve idiot or a lunatic. On the contrary, you are an extraordinarily lucid woman. Staying close demands talents other than sentimentality. Love is like friendship: It needs to be looked after. With a good dose of benevolence (he's been leaving his soaking towel on the floor for twenty years, but you don't even notice it anymore), tolerance (no point arguing about a dentist appointment), doing what you enjoy (you've been away together to romantic Positano six times), compromise (although not too much), and sex (because that is what makes a couple).

GOLDEN RULE:
A lasting relationship is a gift from the gods, but it also requires quite a lot of determination. You know it, you loved it, congratulations! You can be proud of yourself!

Can you fall back in love with the same man?

Parisian Tip

THE BENDS OF THE SEINE

Let the Seine inspire you—as winding as your love, sometimes raging and sometimes flooded, but often serene. Wide at Bercy, narrow at the Quai de Montebello, sometimes deep and sometimes not, green or silvery; it is your reflection, capable of complete transformation, continually changing and eventually arriving, despite obstacles, at the sea. Beauty stretching to the horizon!

Along the journey you have taken together, happy years have been followed by turbulent periods, and you are sometimes shaken by life—and by this vibrating, flirtatious city. We have seen a woman leave her husband after he received a very lewd call from someone unknown, escape into the night, and be found by him in the early morning on the Pont des Arts, venue of their first date, where they fell sobbing into each other's arms. She then fell back in love with him, heart racing as it did in the early days.

We also know you can love the same man all your life because each person is so complex that we can fall in love with their many facets, one after the other. As a young couple, you lauded the originality of this spirited guy. After the children were born, it was his broad shoulders and his ability to cross Paris to the late-night pharmacy to buy medicine for them that moved you. And when the children grew up, his talent for reinventing everyday life enchanted you. "Constancy in love is a perpetual inconstancy which makes our heart attach in turn to all the qualities of the person we love," wrote La Rochefoucauld in his wonderful *Maxims*. Loving all aspects of the other—good and bad—is a secret of a love that endures.

GOLDEN RULE:
The devil is in the details? Happiness too. Book a vacation, weep together at the opera, exchange a gentle and furtive kiss, be moved just at the sound of his voice . . .

EPILOGUE

We didn't agree on everything.

When we first set out, writing a book about love seemed like a fun, lovely, lighthearted thing to do. Later, it felt bizarre, and we felt exposed. We didn't all see things the same way. We realized that each of us is unique and that others might find our perspective disturbing. Luckily, the discussions among us—Eva, who likes to play at being princess; Claire, who leaves no stone unturned to remain hot and keep her marriage in top shape; and Florence, the romantic marshmallow type who is always navigating close shaves—were funny and friendly. So much the better! We responded from the heart, as good friends.

Our words are worth what they are worth, but in the end, whatever you do, remember that the best advice is to follow your own instincts. That is as clichéd as a ride on a Paris tourist boat, but it is true. The proof? All three of us are happy—yet we absolutely disagreed on all the following points.

So we wanted to say to you that it doesn't matter if:

when you discreetly go to the bathroom in the morning, you take the opportunity to brush your teeth

---

you feel like exclaiming "Ugh" at the idea of a sex tape, or if you would love to have a golden shower

---

you are a teenager and put smileys everywhere in your texts

---

you recount your childhood on the first evening, weeping drunkenly on his shoulder

---

you know where the squeegee and the vacuum cleaner are, how to make a béarnaise sauce, and are on the lookout for slippers that are as trendy as Gucci mules you have never wanted to kiss someone else

---

you stroll along all the beaches in France topless

---

you call that guy who never called you back because you never know

---

you like bald men with paunches

---

you flew to Buenos Aires for two days, and in the end it was a wasted trip

---

you sext or have phone sex

---

you say to yourself all day long, "I am madly in love with you, my darling, I've never loved like this, you are the man of my life, my soulmate, my happiness"

---

you don't whisper dirty things when you make love

---

you want to get married the old-fashioned way, with maids of honor in pink

---

you go crazy after having stayed in for a week and you force yourselves to go to a nightclub like two old squares

---

you both put on the same tracksuit to go and jog in the Luxembourg Garden

---

you have your breasts enlarged because deep down you feel more Roman than Parisian

---

you have only one man in your life, or you have a thousand, or you don't have any (yet)

Thanks

A big thank you to Édouard Dutour for his mind, which is unlike any other, and for his intelligence, his communicative joie de vivre, his rare kindness, his mad humor, and his more than careful proofreading.

FLORENCE BESSON thanks . . .

My grandmother (whom I would never have allowed to read this book!), whose love carries me each day, for having taught me to marvel at a poem and the beauty of an apple or a sliver of light in a tree.

My mother, Marie Berrondo Agrell, for her liberty and her elegance at every age. My father, Jacques Besson, who would be proud. My brother and sisters, Paul, Caroline, and Béatrice, for their lifelong encouragement. And their darling children.

My friends, particularly Émilie C., Émilie L., and Laurence S., for their precious friendship and their frankness, which I treasure. But also all the others, for their valuable advice, their laughter, and their affection.

My colleagues at *Elle* and the magazine itself, which is like a family. Very particularly Olivia de Lamberterie but also Sandra Basch and Chantal Lévy. And the journalists Erin Doherty, for her joie de vivre and her "It doesn't matter if . . ." pinched from her *Glamour*, and Santiago Boutan, who left his surfing to come and help us with his vision—so accurate, delicate, and luminous.

My two coauthors and great friends, Eva Amor and Claire Steinlen: We didn't agree about everything, but we did all we could to give good advice to all Parisiennes in love!

Elsa Lafon, for having believed in this book; as well as the whole team at Michel Lafon.

Lionel S., for love, joy, happiness . . . and so much more besides.

And, of course, Gribouille, my super cat, with whom every moment is a delight.

EVA AMOR thanks . . .

Florence Besson, who knows how to manufacture joy and without whom this book would not exist!

Claire Steinlen, five feet, nine inches of smiles and benevolence.

Benjamin Helbert, my sweetheart and superhero.

Mila, my little sugar, still too young to read this book, which will perhaps make her laugh one day.

My father, Max, for his sense of humor, and my mother, Bella, for her sense of love.

My grandmothers, two courageous women, and their husbands—feminists before their time!

My family—uncles, aunts, cousins, Esther, and my little brother, Marc-Élie.

My in-laws, who invented the recipe for brightening up daily life: Jean, Marie-Line, Maxime, Anne-Sophie, Victor, and Clémence.

My friends, with their sharp wits and humor, for all they give me and all we have still to share: Riccardo Beolchi, Charline and Sidney Bouvier, Nicolas Catania, Myriam Delawari, Guillaume Dolisi, Édouard Dutour, Rym El Mati, Elvire Emptaz, Manuel Jeanne, Éléonore Klar, Sophie and Christopher Lalloz, Johann Nouveau, and Émilie Segault; with a special mention for sweet Valérie Dargaud and for Émilie Glavany, my compass.

Philippe Danesi—recommended by Frenchy.

The Paris group who will always be Paris: Marie, Anne-Laure, Antoine, Céline, Claire, Élodie, Fabien, Franck, Jenn, Maeva, Maxime, Ben, Tom, and Agathe.

CLAIRE STEINLEN thanks . . .

Thank you to G., my partner, for having served me all these years as an experimental specimen for the good relationship entomologist I have become thanks to him, but also for his patience and for being so quick on the uptake about when he needed to leave me alone to work, taking the children with him.

Thanks to them too, Achille, Melvil, Alma, and Romy, who put laser sword fights and pillow fights on hold for more peaceful activities.

Thanks to my coauthors, Florence and Eva, for the sushi study evenings in the office and gambas at the Blue Cargo.

Thanks to my mom for the inspiring model of a relationship.

Thanks to stalwarts Capucine Steinlen, Sabrina Bellucci, Karina Si Ahmed, Sandra Teurlay, Emma Joy, Sarah Isal, Nadège Buffe, Vanessa Lalande, Benjamin de Lapparent, PK, and our family psychiatrist, Marc Gabbai, and his muse, Fanny.

And all those men and women who have shared their experiences of relationships and have opened their hearts to me!

THE AUTHORS

FLORENCE BESSON is a journalist for the magazine *Elle*. A report from Iraq, an interview with Hillary Clinton, but above all hours spent talking about love with her Parisian girlfriends! Reciting poems in the early hours on a bench with nightbirds, leaving a nightclub and going straight to church, getting intoxicated by a bridge on the Seine, a tree, a meeting on a Paris roof . . . everything is fuel for her living life as if it were a romantic novel. Too romantic? Absolutely not! Because it makes her happy! Paris is her playground!

EVA AMOR is a lawyer who will never judge you and will always defend you! Work, her guy, her baby . . . She is often in a hurry but always takes the time to advise her friends—single or attached—on love and its surprises and complications. Without principles or morality—but with pertinence and impertinence as a sexy strategist! She gives the brush-off to things that aren't worth it, acts a bit like a princess, and is always ready to laugh at herself—in short, she is such an embodiment of the Parisian woman that she plays the champion of Parisians in love. After all, if your name is Amor . . .

CLAIRE STEINLEN is a journalist for the magazine *Clés* and for the newspaper *Le Télégramme*. Four children—and what about it? She runs all around Paris, to its latest restaurants, its luxury hotels, and its exhibitions—in a minidress to interview Leonardo DiCaprio among others, before returning to the man with whom she is still crazily in love after twenty years together. Author of a book on marriage—*Ten Good (or Bad) Reasons to Get Married*—she knows all about sex toys and children's toys. Lasting love is work. But above all it's a gas. Mama mia!

THE ILLUSTRATOR

photo © Elise Ortious Campion

SOPHIE GRIOTTO began her career in Paris notably by drawing film storyboards for Dior and Jean-Paul Gaultier. Today, she is an internationally renowned illustrator for fashion, advertising, the press, and publishing. She lives with her partner, who is, guess what, a Parisian! They live happily together in the warmth of Sophie's native south. "My eye is attuned to the contemporary woman. By portraying her with the right accessories and attitudes, I accentuate her personality and her originality."